c·r·e·a·t·i·v·e
QUILT CHALLENGES

Take the Challenge
to Discover Your Style & Improve Your Design Skills

Pat Pease and Wendy Hill

C&T PUBLISHING

Text and photography copyright © 2016 by Pat Pease and Wendy Hill

Photography and artwork copyright © 2016 by C&T Publishing, Inc.

Publisher: Amy Marson

Creative Director: Gailen Runge

Editor: Lynn Koolish

Technical Editors: Julie Waldman and Debbie Rodgers

Cover Designer: April Mostek

Book Designer: Christina Jarumay Fox

Production Coordinator: Freesia Pearson Blizard

Production Editors: Alice Mace Nakanishi and Jennifer Warren

Illustrator: Aliza Shalit

Photo Assistant: Sarah Frost

Style photography by Nissa Brehmer and instructional photography by Diane Pedersen, unless otherwise noted

Published by C&T Publishing, Inc., P.O. Box 1456, Lafayette, CA 94549

Library of Congress Cataloging-in-Publication Data

Pease, Pat, 1951- author.

Creative quilt challenges : take the challenge to discover your style & improve your design skills / Pat Pease and Wendy Hill.

pages cm

ISBN 978-1-61745-065-5 (soft cover)

1. Quilting--Technique. 2. Patchwork quilts. I. Hill, Wendy, 1951- author. II. Title.

TT835.P42 2016

746.46--dc23

2015025599

Printed in China

10 9 8 7 6 5 4 3 2 1

DEDICATION

To creative people everywhere: If you want to think outside the box, first you have to believe *there is no box*! Keep making stuff!

~*Wendy Hill*

This book is dedicated to the two men in my life.

First, to my father, John W. James, for all his encouragement and support when I wanted to study art in college. He believed you should get the best tools and supplies you can, and then go for it. He loved my art and quilts, and I wish he were still around to see this book.

And second, to my husband, Jim Pease. Your many adventures with the dogs leave me plenty of time to make quilts and experiment in my studio. I appreciate your support and understanding of my many deadlines and commitments, and your growing tolerance of pins on the floor.

And last, to all the teachers and other quilters I have learned from. I started quilting after my husband and I retired to central Oregon. I think it is difficult to live here and not be a quilter of some sort. The inspiration is everywhere.

~*Pat Pease*

ACKNOWLEDGMENTS

It takes more than a village to write a book, and Pat and I couldn't have done it without the support of our families and friends, the larger quilting community, and the folks at C&T Publishing. You know who you are: Thank you!

Of course, the companies that make all the wonderful products we use to make quilts are very supportive of authors. We'd like to thank the following companies who supported us in the making of our first book together:

- American & Efird
- Aurifil
- C&T Publishing
- Dear Stella
- Fiber on a Whim
- Kreinik
- Oakshott Fabrics
- Quilters Dream Batting
- Ranger Industries
- Sulky of America
- Superior Threads
- Timeless Treasures

Thank you, Pat. In 2008, when we created our first challenge together, we had no idea how the idea of challenge quilts would unfold in our future. The creative process is like a rollercoaster ride, with twists, turns, and surprises. The ride comes to an end, but new rides are always starting: Let's get started on those new challenge ideas!

Thank you, Wendy. I value your friendship more than you know, and it is so nice to have someone around who can finish my sentences and laugh at my jokes. Our next project together sounds like so much fun. We need to get it started.

c·o·n·t·e·n·t·s

INTRODUCTION:
Challenge Yourself

Like most quilters, we live and make quilts in the world of imagination and creativity. When we look through our fabrics at home or go fabric shopping, we don't see yards of whole cloth. Instead, we imagine finished quilts. When we go about our day, we don't *only* see the world around us—we see potential patterns, colors, and ideas for future quilts. When nonquilters say it must take patience to make a quilt, we give our secret smile. Quilters know that doing what you love is an indulgence, not a chore.

The idea to explore our shared affinity for friendship, fabric, and design came naturally to us. We devised a series of challenge themes for the two of us, and we each made a quilt inspired by the theme topic. In addition to our having a lot of fun doing it, one thing led to another and soon we had a special exhibit of our challenge quilts at the Pacific International Quilt Festival in Santa Clara, California, in October 2013. Our exhibit, "A Natural Affinity …," led to this book about our challenge themes, our quilts, and our own exploration of the design process, color, and principles of design.

While we have a lot in common, the way we process information and approach the design process is quite different. Pat is very spontaneous and fearless when it comes to sewing fabric together and cutting it apart again on the way to making a quilt. Wendy takes her ideas and uses structure and organization to get from the beginning to the end. Wendy hates being boxed in by a problem, while Pat sees problems as opportunities to go in another direction. It's this push and pull and give and take that makes it fun for us to share our love of fabric as we develop our individual ideas into finished quilts.

Every time we make a quilt, we have been *inspired by something* to go from idea to finished quilt. When the inspiration is a challenge theme, ideas get focused toward the parameters of the theme while remaining open ended—there are as many ways to respond to a theme as there are quilters. While exploring the themes, we found ourselves more consciously exploring our own personal design process and our own understanding of color and design. When we revealed our quilts side by side, it astonished us how much of our personal style and point of view could be seen in them. At the same time, we each drew upon the same universal considerations of color, value, and design principles common to most artistic adventures.

This book is an invitation to *take the challenge*—by yourself, with a friend, in a small group, or with an entire quilt guild—*using our challenge themes*. We're inviting you to enter the "Land of Color, Design, and Imagination," but we aren't giving you a map. This is not a destination book with actual step-by-step projects. Instead, we're encouraging you to find your own compass using our challenges as the stepping-off points. While navigating the composition, color, and design landscape, you will continue to develop your own style and voice. Along the way, read about our favorite tips and techniques.

Anyone can make a quilt. The first quilt leads to the next quilt, and the next, and the next, until there is no going back. Making quilts becomes a form of self-expression. The more you understand the principles of color, design, and your own personal design process, the better you'll be able to transform your ideas into finished quilts that speak for you.

As a bonus, in Special Techniques (page 86) we share some of the tricks and techniques that we've learned over the years.

~Pat and Wendy

THE CHALLENGES OF
Challenge Quilts

A quick Internet search reveals pages of new, current, and past challenge quilt opportunities ranging from local block and quilt projects to regional contests and large-scale fundraisers. Challenge themes first inspire quilters to respond and then encourage them to stretch their skills and try new techniques. Challenge themes may be narrow or broad in scope, limited to a block or opened up to various sizes of quilts, and may have very few rules or more structured guidelines. There is something for everyone who wishes to participate in a quilt challenge.

As you can imagine, an endless number of challenges can be devised. We selected the ones you see in this book because we found them appealing, inspiring, and focused enough to have cohesion but open ended enough to allow us to run with the idea.

All challenge themes have a focus, including ours, but any good theme is wide open to diverse personal interpretations, as you'll see in our quilts. All challenge themes have rules or guidelines. As you read about the rules and guidelines we used for our challenge quilts, think about how you might want to follow or adapt any part to suit your needs. Below is a list of factors to consider when adapting our challenges or launching your own challenge theme project:

- Define the challenge theme.

- Decide on size limits, if any.

- Make the rules: binding or facing; embellishments or not; limit to conventional quilt materials or allow mixed media; require three layers (with batting) or just two or more layers (with batting optional); and so on.

- Keep the quilt a secret until the end, or allow sharing of work in progress.

- Set one final deadline, break it up into mini-deadlines, or leave open ended.

- Plan the Big Reveal.

The Big Reveal is the surprise culmination of all the time and effort spent in making the challenge quilts. Expect the unexpected as the participants show and tell about how they responded to the challenge theme, with all the twists and turns that led to their finished quilts. Just when you think your own response to the theme *makes the most sense*, you'll be *wowed by the diversity* in the quilts around you. Inspiration is everywhere, and this is especially true at the Big Reveal. You'll want to get started on the next challenge theme right away!

Turn the page and start your quilting adventure with us right now. Challenge yourself to any of these themes, grab a friend, sweet-talk your small sewing circle, lasso your quilt guild to join in the challenge theme fun, or connect with your quilting friends around the world through the Internet. The possibilities are endless.

Reimagine an Old Block

About This Challenge

Many quilters have a favorite traditional block regardless of the kinds of quilts they make. For this challenge, take an old favorite block pattern and adapt it in a new way.

MAKE IT YOUR OWN

Consider the following factors when shaping your own Reimagine challenge:

- Decide whether to make one block or an entire quilt.
- Have everyone contribute one block to a group quilt (for a fundraiser, donation, or gift).
- Have everyone use the same block or allow participants to choose their own.

We decided to adapt our own favorite blocks from the large family of strip-pieced blocks known as Log Cabin. With so many traditional and innovative variations in the Log Cabin category, many quilters say they'd choose this pattern if they could work with only one pattern for the rest of their lives. Wendy chose White House Steps while Pat couldn't wait to work with the Bright Hopes block again.

What did we learn? Exploring the anatomy of a familiar block allows you to go in new directions while being grounded in a foundation that you already understand. Starting with something you understand frees you up to try new things without getting overwhelmed.

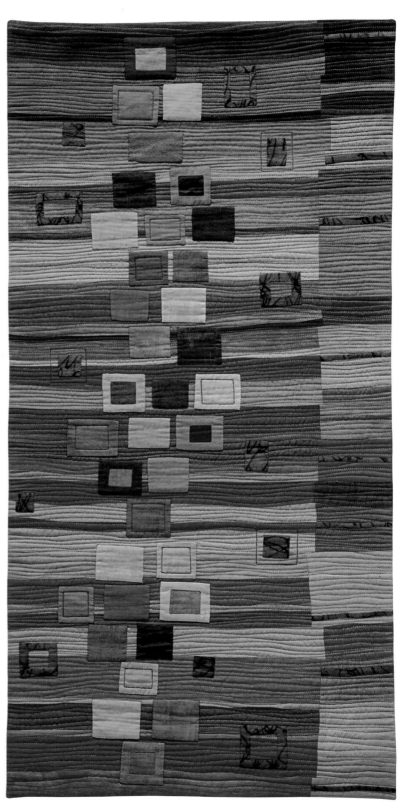

Stepping Out
by Wendy Hill,
19″ × 39″

Wendy deconstructs White House Steps blocks and uses them as the focal point.

with a New Twist

Bright Hopes 2
by Pat Pease,
46″ × 48″

Pat makes Bright Hopes blocks improvisationally
and repeats them for the whole quilt.

PAT'S QUILT:
Bright Hopes 2

**USING BRIGHT HOPES BLOCKS
IMPROVISATIONALLY AND
REPEATING THEM FOR THE
WHOLE QUILT …**

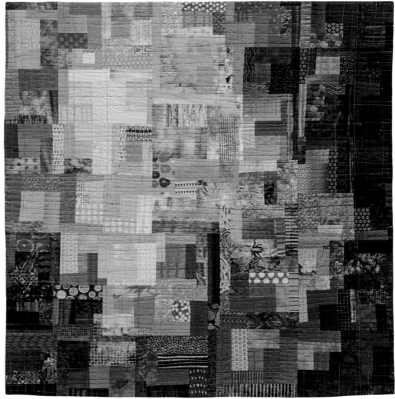

Bright Hopes 2
by Pat Pease,
46″ × 48″

In the Beginning

I love to make the Bright Hopes
block. Wendy showed me how to
make it in 2007, and I have used it
in a number of quilts. One of my
favorites is *Color Study*, done in 2009.

The block is a square surrounded
by four strips of fabric. It is a
simple block to make, though it
does contain a partial seam. As
a nontraditional quilter, I make
blocks that usually don't look like
the ones you find in a how-to
book. I cut pieces of fabric that
resemble squares and strips, but
I don't measure them. I use my
rotary cutter and just eyeball it.

Color Study
by Pat Pease,
quilted by
Tammy MacArthur,
46½″ × 52″

SEWING A PARTIAL SEAM

To make this block, you need a center square and four strips of fabric. Press the seams open after each step.

Sew a partial seam on the first strip.

Add the second strip to the side of the center square.

Trim the second strip.

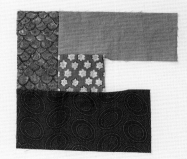

Add the third strip.

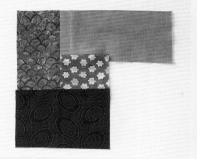

Trim the third strip.

Add fourth strip.

Trim the fourth strip.

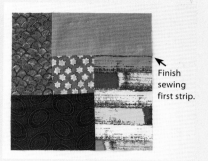

Finish stitching the first seam, joining the first strip to the center square and the fourth strip.

Back side of finished block

Color and Design Decisions

I knew I wanted to make a color-washed quilt, in which one color moves to the next one and the next (in this case, in an analogous color scheme, since the colors are next to each other on the color wheel). The quilt was inspired by the colors of central Oregon in early summer, when the yellow and blue wildflowers first bloom. The sky is always as blue as can be, and the junipers and pine trees are a shiny green after an occasional afternoon thunderstorm. I didn't want a literal representation of the landscape, but rather an impression. I had a color scheme and now the hunt for fabric was on.

Choosing Fabric

Selecting fabric is one of my favorite parts of making a quilt. I look through everything I have, including scraps, because that special piece might be there. I sort all my possible choices into color piles, so when I am making a block, I don't have far to look.

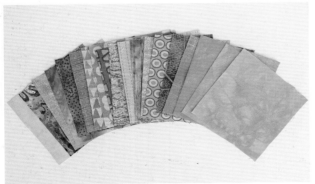

Fabrics sorted by color

I don't worry too much about what kind of fabric I grab, and I like to include silks, linens, and burlaps, if they are the color I need. In fact, I like the variety that the different textures bring to the surface of a quilt. Some of the fabrics I included were more than ten years old, and I like the fact that they don't exactly match current fabrics. Plain fabrics and patterns, large scale and tiny, all go into the mix.

Unstable fabrics

> **TIP**
>
> ### Working with Unstable Fabrics
>
> Silk and other very lightweight fabrics are easier to cut up and sew into a block if they have a fusible knit interfacing applied first. This kind of interfacing is available in white or black, so you can use the white for light-colored fabrics and the black for really dark-colored fabrics. I just follow the directions that come with the interfacing.
>
> If you use heavy linen, burlap, or canvas, it is a good idea to make sure you have large seam allowances, and always (even when you use cotton) press seams open using steam, spritzes of water, and a tailor's clapper. After you try these methods (see Pressing Advice and Seam Treatments, page 94) with your step-by-step pressing, you'll probably never want to go back to the old ways.

Under Construction

In a color wash quilt, the colors flow across the quilt. I start by working on a design wall, putting strips of color in each corner so I know what I am working toward. Then the process of auditioning fabric and analyzing choices begins, as I see what the quilt needs next. I make a few blocks, put them on the design wall, and analyze again.

TIP -

Using the Ultimate 3-in-1 Color Tool

I use the Ultimate 3-in-1 Color Tool (by C&T Publishing; see Resources, page 111) to visualize color progressions, such as chartreuse going to yellow-green, then to spring green, and so on. It also helps me identify tints, tones, and shades in my chosen color families, making it easier to identify fabrics that will fit in.

- -

While I did use quite a few pure colors in my blocks, there are many tints, shades, and tones of my selected colors. As you make blocks for a color wash, remember to work from color to color. Stand back and look at what you have done and then ask what the quilt needs next.

Occasionally I make a block that is not quite right, but if the color isn't too far off, I might leave it. Really wrong color choices stand out, and I use those blocks for something else. Look at your batiks, prints, and hand-dyed fabrics, since they can help when transitioning from one color to another.

Does Block Size Matter?

I try to make my blocks a consistent size, but some may be too small. If this happens, I add another strip of fabric, or maybe even two, to an existing block. Too-large blocks can easily be trimmed. I think blocks for this quilt really can be any size you like. Go ahead and add another strip or two to existing blocks if you need to. Your goal is to sew the blocks together and make the colors flow from one to another.

Adding a strip to make blocks fit together

Quilting

Because *Bright Hopes 2* contains so many colors, I used a multicolored 30-weight thread in the needle and bobbin for the quilting. I also made little thread dots throughout the piece by using a zigzag stitch with the length shortened (see Thread Texturing, Surface Stitching, and Satin-Stitched Triangles, page 100). The dots add little bursts of color throughout. I like the heavy line a 30-weight cotton thread makes, along with the obvious dots.

Why It Works

Bright Hopes 2, as the name implies, is a bright quilt. With an analogous color scheme, the colors move evenly across the quilt, and the variety of fabrics—including patterns, stripes, and solids—helps blur the block pattern as the colors blend but also fade in and out of focus in places. The partial-seam piecing of this block construction also naturally helps blur the seamlines.

Shiny silk and fuzzy linens add texture, and varied fabric patterns draw the viewer in to see what they are.

Last, the heavy, irregular quilting lines repeat the lines of the irregular blocks, and little bursts of color appear here and there throughout the quilt in a subtle way.

The Bright Hopes blocks were a starting point and the underlying foundation for the interplay of color and texture of the surface of the quilt.

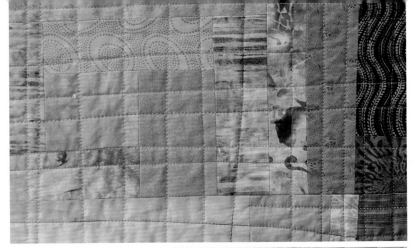

WENDY'S QUILT:
Stepping Out

DECONSTRUCTING WHITE HOUSE
STEPS BLOCKS AND USING THEM
AS A FOCAL POINT ...

In the Beginning

I chose the White House Steps variation of Log Cabin because the concentric-strips block construction appealed to me. While on a three-hour drive, my mind meandered along with the car. My original idea began with deconstructed blocks, but instead of filling the composition with these deconstructions (something I love to do and have done many times), the idea evolved. In this new idea, I could see strips and blocks. With the ideas and feelings fresh and vivid in my mind, I sketched the composition and made notes.

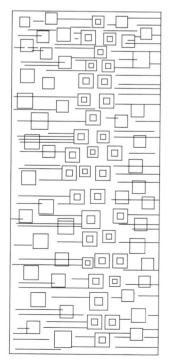

Original sketch

Stepping Out by Wendy Hill, 19″ × 39″

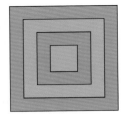

Original White House Steps block, first published around 1895, with the use of alternating light- and dark-value contrasts characteristic of Log Cabin blocks

Whole cloth square A

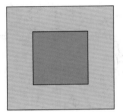

Inset square

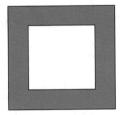

Inside out square C

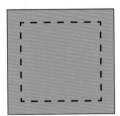

Stitched outline D

Deconstructed White House Steps blocks

Color and Design Decisions

I translate what I see in my mind to the physical world, so you can see it too. Jay Neitz, a color vision researcher at the University of Washington, says, "Color is the silent language of emotion." Choosing fabrics that express your ideas is key to every successful quilt, whether intended for cuddling or for hanging on the wall. If I want to make a baby quilt, I don't gravitate toward somber colors or sophisticated patterns because these colors and fabrics don't speak *baby* to me. Let yourself respond to the color palette, and with each finished quilt you'll develop your own color intuition based on a foundation of knowledge.

From Idea to Fabric

I followed my own "mix, don't match" advice when gathering fabrics for this quilt. Reds, pinks, and oranges in solid-like fabrics kept coming to mind, so I started with this narrow range of colors for the pieced background. I kept adding and subtracting fabrics until I liked the color conversation. I also used fabrics with different fiber contents, surface finishes, and thread counts, such as hand-dyed osnaburg, hand-woven and -dyed fabrics, fabric with a fine/high thread count, high-sheen shot cottons, and assorted linens and silks.

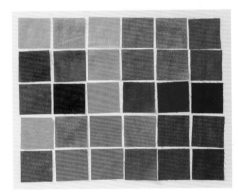

Fabrics for background   Fabrics for squares

TIP -

Color Tips

■ When working with fabrics that are side by side on the color wheel (an analogous color scheme), look for variety in values and venture into other color families for fabrics that help your focus colors shine.

■ When working with a narrow range of colors, use fabrics with assorted fiber contents, surface finishes, and thread counts to add interest in what otherwise could be very dull and monotonous.

■ Add contrasting colors—too much similarity cancels out the color conversation. The odd colors draw attention to and bring out the best in the focus colors. You don't have to love a color/fabric by itself to love how it adds to the color conversation in your fabric assortment.

- -

WENDY'S COLOR NEIGHBORHOOD

The familiar color wheel usually divides the spectrum of colors into 12 or 24 different color families. Anyone who has tried to sort fabrics into neat color piles has probably come across fabrics that defy categorization. That's why I prefer to think of the color spectrum as a neighborhood, where each house is a color family. From the basement to the attic, the values go from dark to light. Nearby houses have closely related color families. Other houses have black and white fabrics, neutrals, or the oddball colors that can't be categorized. When I'm putting together a color scheme, I think about searching the house (all the nooks, crannies, and closets) and going next door, across the street, or across town to find the right color. This imagery helps me get out of the rigid color schemes that come with color wheels.

Under Construction

Line and shape are at the heart of this composition. Lines are continuous marks that define shapes. Shapes, in a variety of sizes, define a space that contrasts with the surroundings. Together, line and shape (with color and value choices) help convey the movement and mood of the composition.

Twists and Turns

Even though most ideas come to me in a full-blown form, the composition evolves as I create the quilt. Forks in the road (decisions) and obstacles (problems) are part of the design process. Pat happily says, "The fun begins when something goes wrong." I grudgingly admit that the unexpected often leads to something better than originally planned.

When I finished piecing the horizontal strips, the panel was not wide enough. I had options: Live with it, start over, or find a way to increase the width. I decided to piece a second, narrow vertical band of horizontal strips. I pieced and added the new vertical band in sections, a few rows at a time. I pieced the new narrow band section, ripped out the seam, sewed the new band right sides together with the quilt top, and sewed the horizontal seam back together. Repeating these steps, I worked my way up the side.

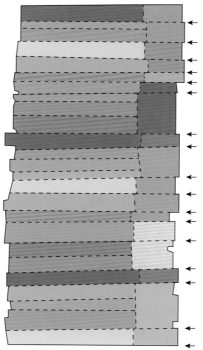

The new vertical seamline, broken up in sections, retains an organic feeling.

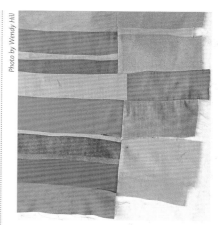

Photo by Wendy Hill

Detail of the process

TIP

Design Ratio

I usually have an overall size in mind when I start a quilt. The most common shapes for quilts are vertical and horizontal rectangles (in a variety of widths and heights) and squares (symmetrical). I often consult Joen Wolfrom's Magic Design-Ratio Tool (by C&T Publishing; see Resources, page 111) when I'm unsure about the shape or design format of the quilt in progress. The pictures of the design formats help you visualize the finished look. A handy chart calculates the dimensions (height and width) for you.

Quilting the Background and Making the Deconstructed Blocks

I didn't want the quilting lines to go through my deconstructed White House Steps blocks, so I quilted the background first, through all three layers (top, batting, fabric backing). After much trial and tribulation, I realized that there was no way to now inset piece the blocks into the already-quilted quilt. The solution was to appliqué the blocks on top. By appliquéing the blocks after the quilting, I also avoided having to stop and start the quilting lines around the appliqué shape.

I made several types of deconstructed blocks, including cut-up whole squares, inside-out squares, and inset squares. I wanted my pieced blocks to float, with a smaller square floating inside a larger square, with no seamlines. Sewing a smaller square into a larger square—called *inset sewing* (see Inset Squares, page 92)—worked perfectly. It takes a little practice, but the effect is worth it.

Pieced unit A

Inset unit B

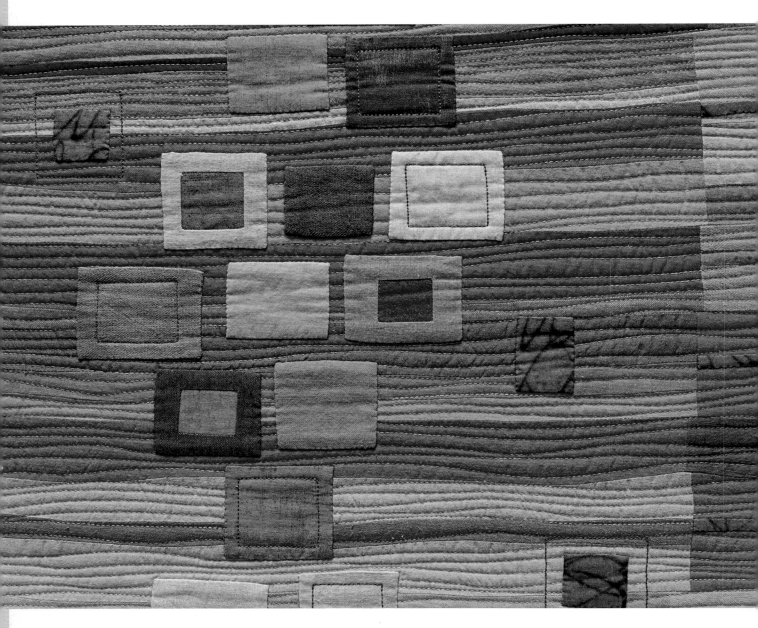

To the Finish Line

I auditioned and appliquéd all the deconstructed White House Steps blocks in place. I use the same invisible blind stitch now (to appliqué and hand sew binding) that my high school sewing teacher taught me ages ago. Blindstitching *hides* the thread running between stitches. This is different from whipstitching (page 95) in which the thread running between stitches is *visible* on the fabric surface. I whipstitch only when the stitching gets covered up in a later step.

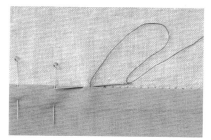

Blindstitching—the thread between stitches is hidden.

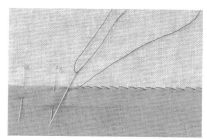

Whipstitching—the thread between stitches is visible on the fabric surface.

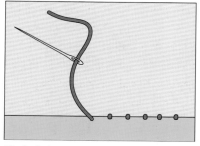

Blind stitch, step 1

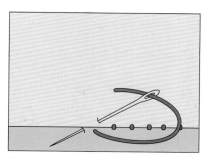

Blind stitch, step 2

Why It Works

When I look at this quilt, I see striations of color and texture that remind me of those found in an exposed cliff with petroglyphs. I also get a sense of movement frozen in time, with the feeling that it will start moving again soon.

The color scheme is dynamic because of the variety of colors, values, and textures that give it a rich and deep glow. The values of the fabrics at the top and bottom of the quilt are quite similar but definitely darker at the top (going against the usual advice), while the middle of the quilt alternates in value—the quilt is balanced but not boringly so.

TIP

Finding the Right Orientation

When I was finished with the quilt, I was not sure which way was up. I spent some time rotating the quilt with each side on top before deciding on the orientation that I thought worked the best. After working on the quilt with the darks at the bottom, I found the composition appeared stronger with the darks at the top. Sometimes rotating the quilt orientation is just the right thing to make a good composition better.

The blocks are integral to the composition. Without them, the background is just another strip-pieced composition that is not balanced—the blue lines on the right-hand side would not be counterbalanced by anything on the left. Without the background, the squares can't exist—they need to be placed on a background. The squares interact with the background, creating a balanced, harmonious whole. The eye is led around the composition in the search for answers. We are curious but not unsettled, and we want to keep looking.

The Value of Value

About This Challenge

Color is a visual language that goes hand in hand with value, the relative lightness or darkness of a color. Both color and value are fluid and relative, shifting depending upon nearby colors and values. A fabric may look darker next to a piece of light fabric but lighter next to a very dark fabric.

Put two fabrics side by side. Just looking at the colors, you might think there is a good contrast or distinction between the two. But if the values are similar, that distinction may vanish. To see the value of colors, look at them in dim light, use a copier or digital camera to convert them to black and white, or use a red or green plastic value lens. You'll discover whether there is real value contrast or not.

Understanding value is important because this is how to make pieced designs apparent, create focal points, suggest dimension, create mood and movement, and allow secondary patterns to be seen. Using value effectively is essential to achieving a quilter's visual goals. This challenge is about making value choices that let the fabrics and the colors communicate the story you want to tell.

ColorBlind
by Wendy Hill,
92″ × 92″

Wendy uses value
to create and play
with pattern.

MAKE IT YOUR OWN

For your Value of Value challenge, consider the following ideas:

- Experiment with a monochromatic color scheme in a range of values from light to dark.

- Choose one block pattern and explore different value placements. Make blocks with different value placements and place them side by side to see the secondary patterns appear.

- Try random value placement, as Wendy did, and see what happens.

- Try using value to evoke a mood in your quilt, as Pat did with her quilt.

Marsh Scene
by Pat Pease,
48″ × 24″

Pat uses value to set the mood.

WENDY'S QUILT: *ColorBlind*

USING VALUE TO CREATE AND PLAY WITH PATTERN ...

ColorBlind
by Wendy Hill,
92″ × 92″

The reverse side of this
quilt is *Color Blinded
Again* (page 60).

In the Beginning

I've always loved the way traditional blocks create secondary patterns when they are placed side by side, depending upon the value placement (lights, mediums, and darks). With these kinds of repeated blocks, the value placement is usually the same in every block. I decided to play with random value placement in the Sawtooth Star block. For the A blocks, I used the classic Double Sawtooth Star pattern. I adapted the Moon and Star Variation pattern for the B blocks, making it a double star too. I couldn't wait to find out what would happen with the stars and secondary patterns.

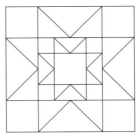

A blocks   B blocks

Color and Design Decisions

The A Blocks

In addition to the random value placement, I also made a variety of stars with three, four, five, or six different fabrics. No matter how many fabrics, I randomly scattered the light, medium, and dark values around the block. No two blocks are alike, with some stars leaping forward, some hanging back, and others blurring.

This Sawtooth Star stands out in stark relief.

This Sawtooth Star hangs back or recedes.

It's difficult to see the Sawtooth Star in this block.

The B Blocks

As much as I love chaos, I knew that without a repeating, alternate B block, the eye would have no place to rest. These blocks use identical black-and-white fabrics with 32 different solid-color and monochromatic (single-color) dotty fabrics.

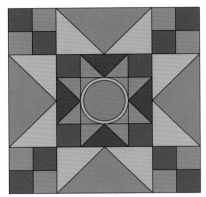

Each of the 32 blocks has a different solid-color and coordinating dotty fabric.

Each B block uses the same black-and-white fabrics. The solid colors and dots are different for each of the 32 blocks.

Samples of alternate B blocks

Chaos and Color, Harmony and Dissonance

This quilt is chaotic and mesmerizing, all at the same time: just the way I like it! The driving force of this design is the seesaw teetering between elements of symmetry versus opposing elements of incongruity. Like other quilt designs on a grid, this symmetrical composition has multiple focal points where the blocks intersect. The random value placement disrupts the usual harmony of grid designs, causing the eye to skitter around, temporarily landing on the somewhat restful black-and-white B blocks before taking off again. This is a visually kinetic quilt that will either win you over or drive you away.

Secondary patterns form when repeated blocks intersect and touch along the sides. With the random value placement, the expected secondary patterns also stand out, recede, or blur depending upon the values located in the adjacent blocks.

Single Irish Chain runs diagonally in both directions with the black-and-white / solid-color checkerboards.

On-point squares form on all four sides where the blocks touch.

Large four-patch squares form at the intersections of the blocks.

Under Construction

Without some tricks up my sleeve, I never would have had the courage to make this quilt. Luckily, there are tools and techniques to make the job easier.

Making Geese Units

Although I made my first quilts with cardboard templates, a no. 2 pencil, and scissors, I'm grateful those dark days are over. I used the Small Flying Geese Ruler 3″ × 6″ (by Quilt in a Day) to make my geese units in sets of four. There are many ways to construct a goose (unit) and probably unlimited ways to use the geese rectangles, as quilters across the decades into the present have shown.

Flying Geese blocks

Bias-Covered Circles

For the traditional Moon and Star Sawtooth Star block, the raw-edge circle (moon) is zigzag stitched to the background block. By covering the raw edge of the circle with self-made bias tape, you get to add another fabric to the mix. Machine topstitch (or hand blindstitch as I did) the bias tape in place for a professional finish.

TIP

Assembly-Line Sewing

When making a repeated block, set up an assembly line to group similar tasks together. This economy of motion saves a lot of time when making repeated blocks while also letting you focus on the same type of task over and over.

Reversible Quilts and Reversible Double French-Fold Binding

While doing all the assembly-line sewing to make the 64 blocks for this quilt, I decided to make it reversible. Read more about how I put the two sides together in Making Quilts Reversible (page 64). When I started making reversible quilts, I wanted to have reversible double-fold binding too. My method is simple, but the formula must be adjusted to accommodate the thickness of your quilt and the seam allowance of the binding (see Reversible Double-Fold Binding, page 86).

Why It Works

This quilt works for me because I intended to have a visually kinetic quilt. Whether or not you like this busy, vibrant quilt, I used sound color and design decisions to get this result: The multicolor (polychromatic) color scheme includes a range of values, pure hues, tints, tones, and shades. This quality, along with the large variety of fabrics, adds complexity to the overall look. The random value placement alters how the stars and secondary patterns come forward, recede, or blur. This quilt exemplifies the saying "Color gets the credit, but value does the work."

PAT'S QUILT: *Marsh Scene*

USING VALUE TO SET THE MOOD ...

Marsh Scene by Pat Pease, 48″ × 24″

In the Beginning

I grew up in Wisconsin, where there are many fresh-water streams, lakes, and marshes. In the summer these are lovely places to swim, canoe, and explore, and in the colder months they have their own unique beauty. Skies darken as thousands and thousands of migrating water-fowl pass through the area, bringing out the hunters. My father was an avid bird hunter, as my husband is today. Both have told me that the birds get moving when the weather gets bad. Stormy weather gets the birds moving, as they search for a better spot to be.

I decided to make a small quilt that represented a marsh with an impending storm—I had seen plenty of them growing up. I'd also seen photos my husband had taken in the Pacific Northwest. Colors are muted, dark, and gray, as the sun sometimes fights the clouds to come out.

Color and Design

Almost any kind of fabric can work when you are doing a landscape quilt—I usually use batiks, solid-color cottons, and hand-dyes. Subtle patterns and stripes are also useful.

Almost all of the colors in *Marsh Scene* have one thing in common—they are not pure colors. To help tell my story, I chose colors that are shades, in which black has been added to darken the color, and tones, in which gray has been added to soften the color. A few tints, where white has been added to lighten a color, appear in the sky and water, but even these have an icy feel. There isn't a lot of life around a marsh in winter, and fabric choices need to reflect that.

What is most important in setting the scene of this quilt is value. Using values that are close together in both the sky and the marsh presents a solid-looking, gloomy vision of the landscape—there is no sun-dappled land or blue sky punctuated with white, fluffy clouds; rather, it feels cold and unmoving, like a storm is coming.

The strong value contrast between the sky and the marsh delineates the sky from the land and reinforces the landscape feel.

Under Construction

For a soft, natural look, I made the quilt using torn strips of fabric that vary from about ½″ to 2″. I premade the quilt sandwich by fusing the backing fabric to the batting and then spraying the other side of the batting with temporary adhesive spray so I could place the strips of fabric directly on the batting. Using a variety of fabrics (cottons, linens, and silks) and leaving the frayed edges helped blend together the strips. Working on my design wall, I blocked out areas for the sky, water, and land, continuously auditioning fabrics and eliminating those that were too bright. I also used the reverse side of some printed fabrics because these backs had a nice muted quality.

I continued to add strips until I was happy with the composition and the mood of the piece.

Torn strips

Quilting Slowly and Carefully

With my walking foot attached to my machine, I slowly stitched down all the fabric strips horizontally across the quilt. I used threads that mostly matched the fabrics, but some don't, and that was a deliberate choice. I tried not to stitch the strips completely down because I wanted there to be lots of texture and fraying of the fabric. In some areas you can see only a tiny edge of the fabric, while in others you can see the whole strip. In a few places you see only the fringe of the fabric. These treatments are intentional. I feel they add to the depth of the piece and draw the viewer in to see what they are. Finally, I quilted over the piece again to make sure everything would stay where I wanted it to be.

Finally ... Scissors and a Rotary Cutter

To create the details, I cut out some hunters and ducks, and fused them in place. The thin strips of fabric are reeds, grasses, and cattails. In the sky, I placed birds on top of birds, in an attempt to show motion and to create a larger flock of ducks. Decoys placed by the hunters float along the surface of the water, drawing the ducks in toward the hunters. They add more detail to the piece and again draw the viewer in to see what they are.

Edge Treatment

I left the raveled edges in place as they were—any sort of binding or edge treatment would change the character of the piece. In certain areas, fabric strips go off the edges, contributing to the natural subject matter.

Why It Works

While color helps to set the tone, with pale icy tints for the sky and muted colors for the marsh, it is value that is key. Using colors that are close in value for the sky presents the overcast, gloomy, leaden feeling of an impending storm. The muted marsh fabrics that are close in value make it hard to distinguish specific features of the marsh, except for the grasses that contrast in both value and direction (the marsh is horizontal; the grasses are vertical). But the value contrast of the grasses with the marsh is not nearly as strong as it would be on a bright sunny day.

The horizontal nature of the composition is emphasized by the torn strips of fabric and the strong horizon line, but the reeds and grasses offer contrast and help to move the eye up and down across the quilt. The same is true of the ducks in the sky and the decoys in the water, giving the viewer a reason to look all around the quilt.

Unlikely Materials

About This Challenge

While going through a large garbage bag of donated fabrics, Pat found a fabric she'd never seen before: hair canvas interfacing. This woven interfacing, used in tailored garments, is a beautiful mix of animal, natural, and/or synthetic fibers. Wool and goat hair is a commonly used combination, but we've seen camel and horsehair fibers mixed with rayon, viscose, and polyester. Higher percentages of animal hair equate with more beautiful striations and tints in the woven fabric (and a more expensive product).

For our challenge, we had to use a significant amount of hair canvas interfacing, as well as any other *unlikely* materials we wanted to add. We agreed to define *unlikely* in our own way, but we both included fiber contents or fabric styles not usually used with quilts. In the past few years, we've both been drawn to coarsely woven fabrics (hemp or linen burlap, osnaburg), fabrics with different surface textures (shiny, silky), and other fabrics besides quilting cottons. This challenge gave us a reason to try these fabrics out. For your challenge, you decide how to define *unlikely materials* or try using hair interfacing for yourself.

Snow Strings
by Pat Pease,
37″ × 57″

Pat uses a monochromatic color scheme to incorporate the unlikely material.

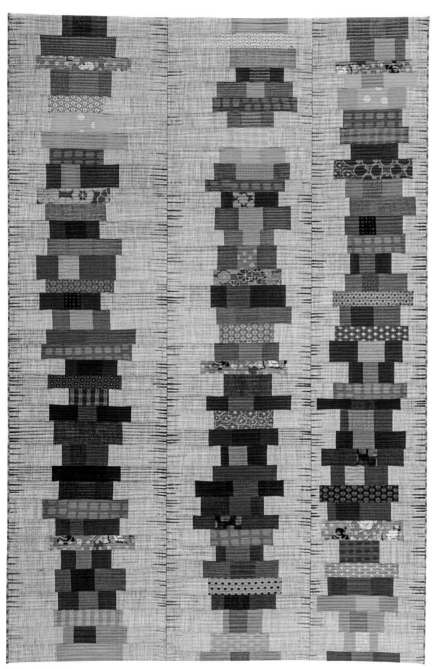

MAKE IT YOUR OWN

- Go outside your comfort zone and try new-to-you materials. These will vary depending upon what you usually use.

- Use a paper bag to exchange one or more unlikely materials, which will be kept secret until the Big Reveal.

- Use hair interfacing for yourself, as we did with our quilts.

Cairn Study 3
by Wendy Hill,
34″ × 53″

Wendy uses color to accentuate the unlikely material.

PAT'S QUILT:
Snow Strings

USING A MONOCHROMATIC COLOR
SCHEME TO INCORPORATE THE
UNLIKELY MATERIAL ...

In the Beginning

During the winter of 2014, the Pacific
Northwest was hit by a major snow-
storm. Areas of Oregon that rarely
get snow had significant amounts,
and the area I live in received more
than two feet in two days. I was
trapped inside my home, unable to
get out even to collect the news-
paper or mail. I keep a small flock
of chickens that need daily tending,
so each morning I would bundle up
and head out to make sure they were
still alive. I would trudge through the
drifts, snow up to my waist, making a
crude path to the chicken coop. After
a few days, the snow stopped and
the path became easier to follow.
I noticed the layers and layers of
snow on the sides of my path, and
this became the inspiration for *Snow
Strings*. Bits of vegetation, dirt, and
birdseed were stuck in these layers,
and the colors within the layers were
often very different. Oh, they were
mostly white, but many were not.

Snow Strings by Pat Pease, 37" × 57"

Color and Design Decisions

When you decide to make a quilt that is mostly white, or any other single color (called a *monochromatic* color scheme), shades, tints, and tones of that color become very important. If you don't pay attention to the values you are using, your quilt will look flat and likely uninteresting (see The Value of Value, page 18). Go to a fabric store and look at all the fabrics that are all or mostly white. I am sure you will be surprised at how many there are. You will find creamy whites and really pure bright whites, along with whites that have many other colors included. Texture is also important and can help move the eye around a quilt.

Unlikely Materials

Since this was the Unlikely Materials challenge, I was able to look for all types of fabrics that are in the stores that you would not usually put in a quilt. Hair interfacing was a must, though it can be difficult to work with. By using an extra-wide seam allowance, I was able to keep most seams fairly flat. Since the challenge is to think outside the quilting fabric box, ask yourself, "Can this material be cut up and can I stitch through it with my machine?" Because this quilt would never be washed, I collected acid-free paper, along with linens, toweling, cross-stitch fabric, silk and silk blends, linens, osnaburg, and a number of utility fabrics, such as drapery linings, muslin, and the like. All they had to be was white, or almost white. I even included some lightweight embroidered cotton that is a decorator item.

Assorted unlikely materials

Likely Materials

We had agreed that is was okay to use some likely materials in this unlikely challenge, and they help to hold all the other materials together. I used stylized patterns to represent snowflakes, and striped and lined fabrics to represent layers of snow. When pulling together fabrics, I often look at the reverse, or wrong side, of materials to see what they are like. I am often surprised by what I find—the muted printed patterns are sometimes just what I need.

Likely materials

Check out the reverse side of fabric; sometimes it's perfect.

Under Construction

Sewing together unlikely materials can be challenging because the fabrics range from stiff to very delicate. An extra-generous seam allowance makes sewing easier and allows you to get the seams to lie flat. A wooden clapper and plenty of steam from your iron are often necessary (see Pressing Advice and Seam Treatments, page 94). Test these materials separately to find the best handling technique. It is also a good idea to be careful when you are pressing delicate silks and papers, which can be easily scorched. A pressing cloth can help to prevent unwanted burn marks.

Putting It All Together

This is where the auditioning and exploring takes place. I simply sew sections of fabric together and then play with them on the design wall. It is a spontaneous process of what looks good with what. Stand back and analyze what you have done. Ask yourself questions. Do you need more texture or color? Are the materials doing what you want them to do? Move things around and don't be afraid to cut fabric up, because it can always be sewn back together. Is there balance? Try putting new fabric up on your design wall to see if there is a better choice to be made. A reducing glass can really help with this process because it allows you to see your whole quilt.

Quilting Choices

Most of the time I like my quilting lines to be obvious to the viewer, and to do this I use heavy-weight thread. When I make a string quilt, I like to repeat the shapes of the strings, so straight-line quilting works best for me. It may be simple, but it can be very effective. In *Snow Strings* I used silk, cotton, and rayon thread. One thread was variegated creams and whites, and may be visible only to those who view the quilt up close. Heavy stitching lines are, of course, more visible from far away and can help to add texture to the quilt.

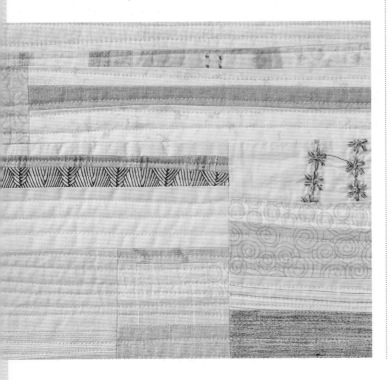

Finishing Choices

The last decision I had to make was whether to put a binding on *Snow Strings* or to use a facing treatment instead. Because of all the unlikely materials I used, this quilt is thin in some areas and quite thick in others. Getting a binding to lie flat and have square corners would be difficult, and I needed a treatment that would help to get the bulk out of the corners. When you put a facing on a quilt (see Facing Finish, page 88), the corners get trimmed, and this was what was needed. I was also concerned that if I used a binding treatment, even a white one, I would have two long vertical lines on either side of the quilt that would conflict with my idea of layers and layers of snow.

Why It Works

Collecting unlikely materials was so much fun, but incorporating them into a quilt was the difficult part. I didn't want to just throw them on the quilt; I wanted them to help tell the quilt's story. They had to have a purpose, not just be there. Many of the "unlikelies" are heavily textured, adding depth to the quilt. Some just draw the viewer in to see what they are and help to move the eye across the quilt.

An all-white quilt depicting snow could have been quite dull, but *Snow Strings* is anything but that. If you look at snow, you see many different colors, not just white. There are shadows, layers of shiny ice, broken crusts, and debris of all sorts to be found. I used many colors other than pure white or a light color to show something that is white. Patterns in the fabric represent stylized snowflakes, but you have to come in close to observe then. Shiny silks and frosted fabrics add that icy look, something you would want in a snow scene. Also, there are several fabrics that represent vegetation, something you also would expect to see outdoors. Striped fabrics look like layers, as does the seersucker fabric I used. These selected fabrics are doing a lot of work for me. I used very little pure white, but it still reads as a white quilt. And last, there is repetition—the linear quilting reinforces the linear effect of the string of fabric. This quilt definitely tells a story of layers of snow on a cold day.

WENDY'S QUILT:
Cairn Study 3

USING COLOR TO ACCENTUATE THE
UNLIKELY MATERIAL ...

In the Beginning

In a 2011 I made a quilt using red
and red-orange pieces of zippers
called *SummerTimeBlues* (page 34).
Intrigued by the stack of red and
red-orange zipper chunks, I made
Cairn Study (page 34), with the
stacks of zipper pieces and the
ghost stacks. I couldn't get the
idea of stacks out of my mind. I
wondered what would happen
with a lot of smaller stacks, which
led to *Cairn Study 2* (page 34). Two
years later, the Unlikely Materials
challenge got me thinking about
stacks again. I didn't start out to
make a series of quilts on this
theme, but that's what ended up
happening.

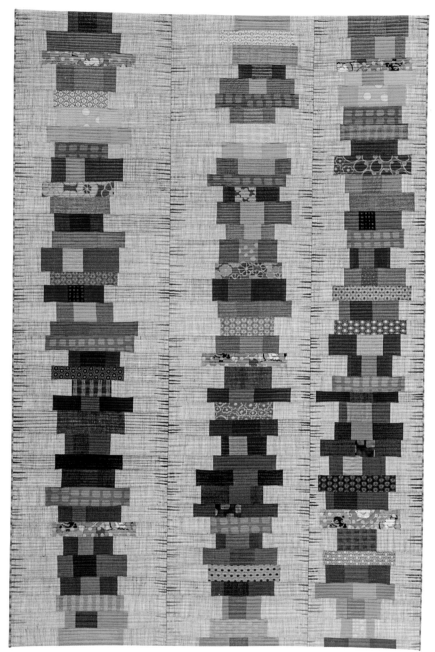

Cairn Study 3
by Wendy Hill,
34" × 53"

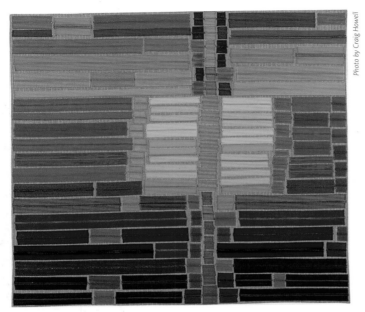

SummerTimeBlues
by Wendy Hill,
22″ × 20″

I loved the stack of red and
red-orange cut-up zippers.

Cairn Study
by Wendy Hill,
16″ × 31½″,
from the collection of
Susan and Craig Howell

The same idea of a stack as seen in
SummerTimeBlues, but in a new way

Cairn Study 2
by Wendy Hill,
38½″ × 20¾″

Individual stacks of
frayed shot cotton
squares

Color and Design Decisions

An Emotional Color Wheel

At first glance, the stacks might appear to be a full color wheel, but they're not. While the colors do run together in a spectrum, key colors from a full color wheel are missing. I auditioned fabrics over and over to find the versions of each color that would evoke a warm and glowing feeling against the hair canvas interfacing. The fabrics had to relate to each other and to the hair interfacing to stay in the mix. Key lesson: Don't try to guess how the fabric mix will look. It takes concrete trials and many failures to get the color conversation going in the direction you want.

I used three types of hair interfacing in the neutral strips: one from 1986, leftovers from making a Pendleton wool coat; one goat hair mix; and one primarily wool.

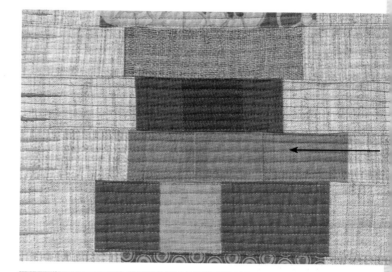

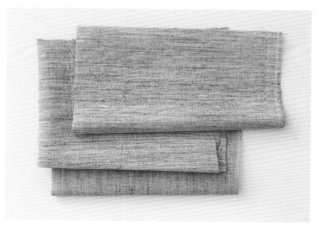

Hair interfacing samples

A Color Conversation

Each column began with identical colors of shot cottons in exactly the same order but cut into rectangles of various sizes. These formed the backbone of the stacks and the overall design. Each column evolved as I inserted prints, woven fabrics, and so on into the mix. Follow the same shot cotton in all three stacks and notice how the surrounding fabrics affect the appearance of the same color shot cotton.

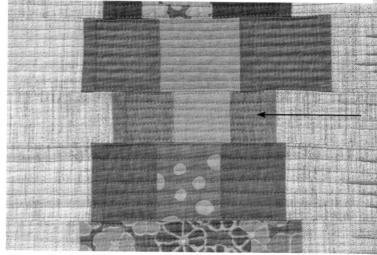

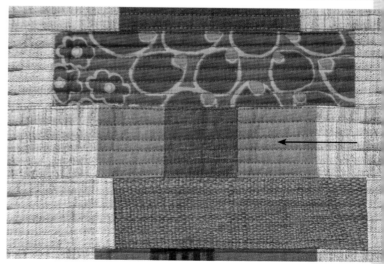

Other fabrics in this mix include hand-dyed hemp burlap; synthetic paper; linens and linen blends; shot cottons, silks, rayons, linens, and blends; silks and silk blends; Oakshott Fabrics striped shot cottons; rayons and rayon blends; tulle; acetate (and other synthetics); and woven, printed, and specialty cottons.

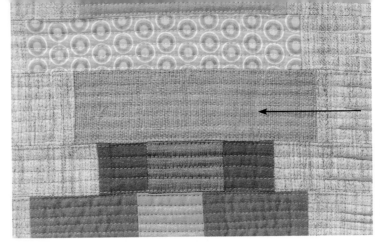

Hand-dyed hemp burlap

TIP

Using the Right Materials for the Quilt

We all have colors and styles that appeal to us, but try to avoid preconceived ideas or favorites when searching for the right color, fabric, material, design element, and so on. For example, I almost never use acetate in anything I make, yet I found acetates with just the right color and sheen. I desperately wanted to use zippers in this quilt, but the quilt kept saying no. I had to listen!

- -

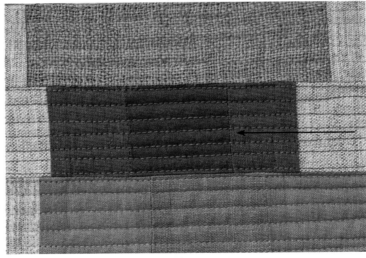

Synthetic paper

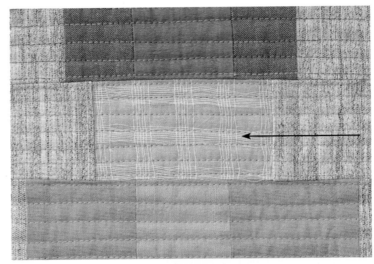

Oakshott Fabrics shot cotton

Tulle overlay

Under Construction

I constructed this quilt in three panels. Typically this construction trick (the seamlines in the background disappear) creates an illusion that the irregular colorful stacks are coming forward or floating (positive space) against a uniform neutral background (negative space). I purposely forced the neutral background to alternate in the foreground with the colorful stacks. The three colors of neutrals, the quilting, and the satin-stitched triangles all work together to help the neutrals form their own stacks instead of receding quietly into the background.

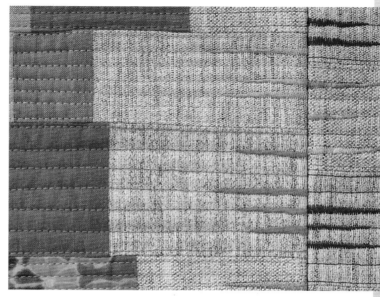

Narrow, roughly parallel quilting lines and satin-stitched triangles bring the background forward.

Auditioning and Cutting the Fabrics

I live by the saying, "If you don't have time to do it right, when will you have time to do it over?" and I hate getting boxed in unnecessarily by a problem. But when I plan ahead, I'm not just problem solving. I'm also exploring options in my mind instead of forging ahead with cutting and sewing.

I set up strings on my design wall to mark the sides and centers of each column. The strings also helped in two other ways. The string down the middle of each column helped me position the rectangles of shot cottons, prints, and woven fabrics, including the little rectangles found in many of the strip units. The strings marking the outside edges of the columns showed me how to cut the interfacing to the right sizes. By the time I had this figured out, I was ready to cut fabrics with abandon.

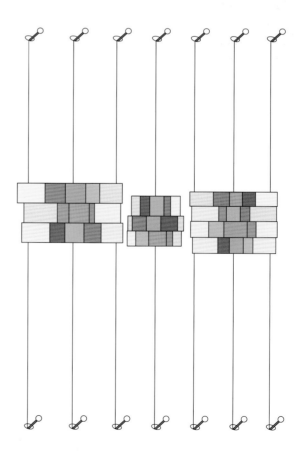

Quilting and Satin Stitching as You Sew

Hair canvas interfacing (like any canvas) is stiff. I planned to quilt in closely spaced parallel lines ending in satin-stitched triangles, matching the thread color to one of the fabrics in the rectangle unit in *each* column. Quilting this piece as a whole quilt would have been a nightmare with the bulk and all the thread tails of the stops and starts of the closely spaced quilting lines. My own quilting-as-you-sew methods (pages 95 and 97) came about in response to solving these kinds of problems.

Because the columns were narrow, it was easy to quilt each one individually. I backstitched in the seam allowance, eliminating the need to deal with thread tails. After marking the seam and cutting lines on the long sides of each column, I satin stitched the triangles (see Satin-Stitched Triangles, page 102) at the ends of most, but not all, of the quilting lines. After sewing the quilt right sides together (with a wide seam allowance), I covered the pressed-open seams on the back with self-made seam covers.

Finishing the Edges

After the quilt was finished and hanging on a wall, the stiffness of the hair canvas interfacing wasn't a problem. But while I was constructing the quilt, the stiffness presented some challenges, including finishing the outside edges.

The top and bottom edge folded over with a facing just fine, but the sides refused to fold over, not even one tiny bit. I tried binding options with no success. I'd gotten this far with advance planning, but now I had to deal with this unexpected problem. There are always answers: I faced the top and bottom edges and satin stitched the two vertical sides (see Professional-Looking Satin-Stitched Edge Finish, page 99). I could not have planned it any better!

Seam on the front

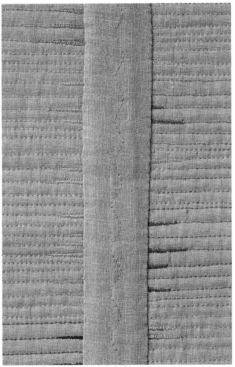

Seam cover on the back

Faced top edge

> **TIP**
>
> ### Sometimes It's the Little Things That Count
>
> Looking at the quilt photo (page 29), block out the stitching between the columns with your finger and you'll see how much the quilting and satin-stitched triangles add to the composition. Sometimes a simple solution makes all the difference.

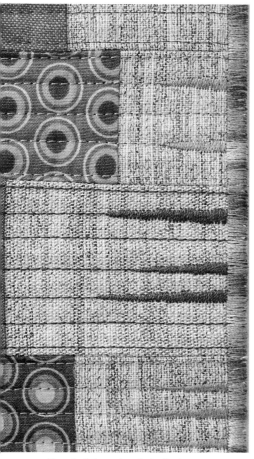

Detail of the satin-stitched edge

Why It Works

The various hair interfacings have unique colors and textures not present on other fabrics. I also incorporated other unlikely materials that add to the overall texture, color, and look of the quilt. With any quilt, it's a good thing when the long-distance view pulls you in and then, as you move closer, you notice little details. In this case, when you get pulled in, you discover not only the hair interfacings but burlap, synthetic paper, tulle, and more. I never want these things to stand out by themselves. Rather, I want the materials used to be secondary to the overall composition; otherwise, it's more of a stunt than anything else.

I also put my own spin on this type of composition. As my third quilt exploring the concept of stacks, it made sense for this quilt to be the most complex. This composition swings back and forth, not quite one thing or another: balanced but also teetering, symmetrical but irregular, congruent but dissonant. Humans want to find balance and symmetry, but we don't want the search to be too easy or too hard.

- There are three columns (balance), but the columns and the neutral spaces between them are not all the same width (imbalance). Instead, the actual vertical center is to the left of the center of the middle column. The right-hand column is the narrowest. There is a balance because (1) there is an odd number of columns and (2) the left-hand column is the widest, so in a teeter-totter way, it balances. But then, the middle and right columns start to tip the teeter-totter. Then it balances up again. Then it tips.

- The pieced strips share a uniform rectangular shape (symmetry), but the varied heights of each strip unit and varied widths of the colored fabrics throw off the eye (irregularity).

- The smaller rectangles of colored fabric run up the middle of the columns (balance), but these little shapes run mostly off center (irregularity).

- The background neutrals blend to form a unified color (congruence). The colored quilting lines and satin-stitched carrot shapes force the background forward (dissonance). It's a bit of an optical illusion, with the colorful stacks and the neutral background fighting for dominance.

Pass It Back and Forth

About This Challenge

For this collaborative challenge, I started a quilt and gave it to Pat without telling her anything about my ideas or intentions. At the same time, Pat started a quilt and gave it to me without telling me anything about it. We continued this process of passing the quilts back and forth, sometimes with raw materials, *always without speaking*, until one of us declared a quilt was finished. We each had the freedom to do anything to the quilt at any time, including scrapping it and starting over.

We were inspired by the way twin sisters Lisa and Lori Lubbesmeyer work together in this manner on their fiber art pieces (lubbesmeyer. com). Pat and I don't have their special telepathic twin-speak, but we wanted to experience this process for ourselves. I had no qualms about Pat's cutting up my quilt—and you know she did at every opportunity—but I didn't want to disappoint her with the changes I made. Pat felt the same way, hoping I would like what she did. We plan to do more of these collaborative challenges. We highly recommend this kind of challenge, either as described or altered to fit your needs.

Silent Reflection
by Wendy Hill and Pat Pease,
57½" × 22"

Using repetition to unify the elements in one quilt

and Do Not Speak

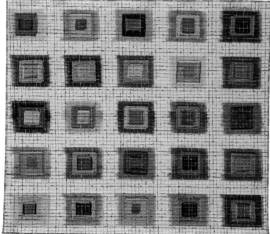

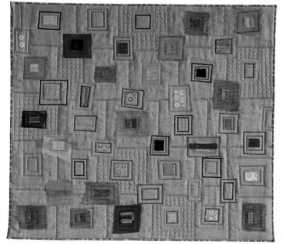

MAKE IT YOUR OWN

Consider these factors:

- Be prepared to let go of control of the outcome and grow a thick skin as you watch your work get altered—this is excellent practice for making dispassionate evaluations of your own work.

- Remember this challenge is more about the process than the results (finished quilts).

- Look at the piece to get grounded (with the principles of color and design) before adding to or subtracting from the quilt in progress. Don't just cut or rip for the *shear* fun of it.

Square Dance
by Pat Pease and Wendy Hill,
triptych, each about 18″ × 18″

Using repetition to unify the elements in a triptych

WENDY'S QUILT:
Silent Reflection

USING REPETITION TO UNIFY THE ELEMENTS IN ONE QUILT …

Silent Reflection by Wendy Hill and Pat Pease, 57½" × 22"

Round 1:
Wendy Starts the Quilt

I started the quilt with a background of raw edge–pieced and thread-textured hair interfacing, and sent it off to Pat neatly rolled up with some optional materials.

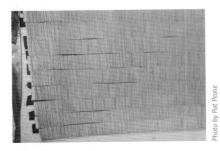

Photo by Pat Pease

Photo by Wendy Hill

Round 2:
Pat Cuts It Apart

Pat explores an idea by doing—actually cutting and sewing—in a process of adding and subtracting, multiplying and dividing. She has no fear about burning bridges or being backed into a corner. In doing this, Pat asks what-if questions, tries out ideas, edits, makes changes, and so on. In contrast, I am much more likely to explore options by sketching and imagining first, before actually cutting fabrics. Either way, this trial and evaluation is key to successful quilt compositions.

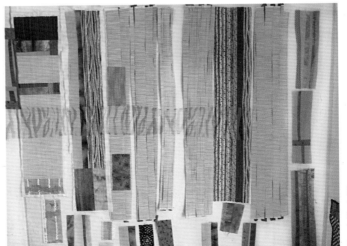

Photo by Wendy Hill

Pat cuts and sews over and over to make units.

Round 3:
Wendy Sews It Back Together

This challenge forced me to improvise each time I got the quilt back. I added more units and started sewing the quilt back together in a vertical format. I could see an abstract landscape coming together.

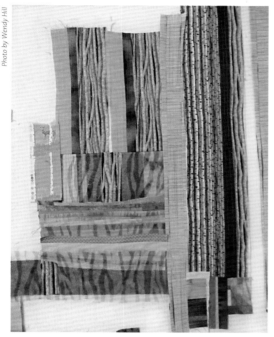

In progress

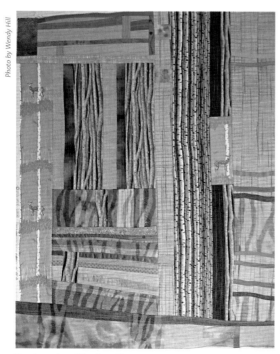

Ready to hand back to Pat

Round 4:
Pat Cuts It Apart—Again

Pat "confided" to an audience (and me) that she planned to cut up the quilt again (so much for no talking). Oh yes, Pat cut it up and put it back together in a narrow, horizontal composition (in three sections). She had doubts about it, but I thought she was onto something.

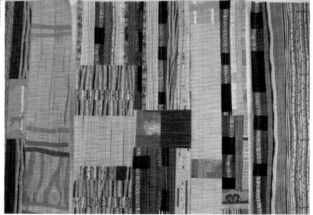

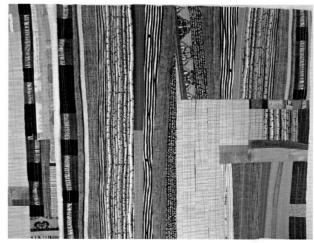

Big inverted L shape jumps out

Round 5: Wendy Cuts and Reassembles the Quilt

In Round 3, I liked the direction of my abstract landscape in a chunky vertical rectangle (roughly a 3:4 aspect ratio). But with the addition of new fabrics and Pat's narrow horizontal shape, the composition packed the punch of a vibrant panoramic scene.

Unlike Pat, I can't just start cutting up a quilt, at least not without getting sick to my stomach. Instead, I printed photos of the three panels on copier paper and *cut these up!* Satisfied with my final mock-up, I reproduced the steps with the real quilt. When Pat agreed the quilt was finished, I finished the outside edges with a facing (see Facing Finish, page 88).

I cut out about 9″ from the total width while consolidating the image into a tighter composition. I added more texture-on-texture by collaging different areas of birch trees together in one place.

When I stepped back from the design wall, the big inverted L shape jumped out at me. I cut and rearranged that area to get rid of the distracting L. In other places, I inserted some of the leftovers back into the composition.

Pat included a long half-zipper, so I added two more half-zippers to balance it out. From several feet away the viewer just sees colors, colors and patterns. Up close, the zippers add an element of surprise (see Using Zippers in Your Quilts, page 103).

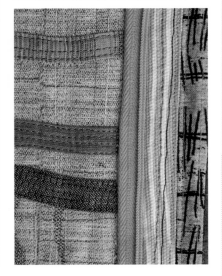

TIP ....

Trial and Evaluation

- Use photocopied prints for the trial and evaluation phase of the design process—you can cut and experiment without worrying about using real fabric. With trial and evaluation, you assess the relative merits of the changes according to your intuition and your growing foundation of color and design knowledge.

- Take photos as you alter and experiment. You'll need to be able to re-create the steps with the actual quilt.

....

USING WIDER SEAM ALLOWANCES

Since we started with collaged fabric stitched to batting, we carried on with this method of stitching (see Quilting-As-You-Sew to Batting, page 97) throughout the construction process. We used a wider seam allowance and always pressed the seams open (see Pressing Advice and Seam Treatments, page 94). It was easy to cut apart, rip out seam allowances, or add more quilted units as Pat cut things apart and Wendy put them back together.

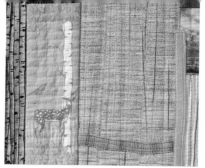

Why It Works

In the drive to make meaning of what they see, viewers take in the long, narrow format along with the other visual clues and conclude it's a landscape of sorts. On closer examination, the details don't match literal landscape features. Yet the mood and feelings of an abstract landscape persist. The (almost) 3:1 aspect ratio opens the door to understanding this quilt in a way that my original vertical format never could.

Pat and I both follow a mix-don't-match philosophy as we gather eclectic assortments of fabrics. Pat buys on speculation while I tend to collect fabrics for a specific quilt. We advise mixing it up when gathering fabrics. Start with fabrics from your stash or scraps to get the collection started. Swap fabrics with a friend to get your hands on things you don't normally buy. Shop across the store from a mix of designers, styles, and colorways. Imagine the squeals of delight when Pat and I discovered a display of "tulle on a spool" in a local fabric store. We did not know then that the zebra-striped tulle would be perfect in an abstract landscape quilt.

Your final collection will have a unique range of colors and styles.

The quilt includes many styles of fabric: abstract, representational, batik, ethnic, geometric, striped, plaid, novelty print, solid, and so on.

Fabrics that have irregular, random, non-repeating, and more chaotic patterns

It's a good idea to vary the scale of the prints in any given composition.

Fabrics with distinct motifs that contrast with the background

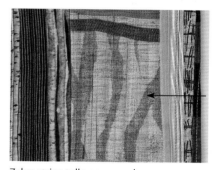

Zebra stripe tulle-on-a-spool

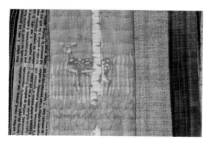

Motifs that are isolated against the background

Repetition is key to the success of this design. Seeing this quilt is like hearing variations of a melody performed in a musical piece. We see repetition in the variations of the lines, shapes, values, colors, patterns, textures, and so on. The proportions of elements add to the harmony, direction, focal points, and balance as the eye moves around. This quilt is captivating.

Tree prints (there are also stripes and other prints with ordered/regular patterns)

PAT'S QUILT:
Square Dance

USING REPETITION TO UNIFY THE ELEMENTS IN A TRIPTYCH ...

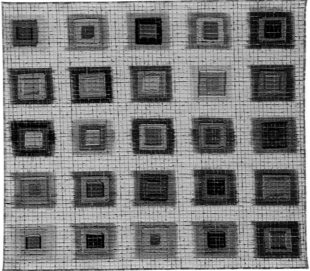

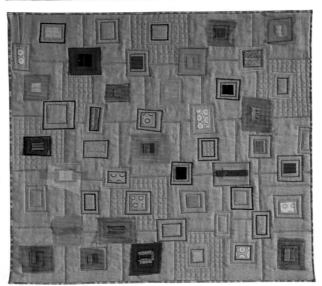

Square Dance, triptych by Pat Pease and Wendy Hill, each about 18″ × 18″

Round 1:
Pat Starts the Quilt

I gave Wendy an 18″ square quilt top with fused squares that I had started in a workshop with Sue Benner (Fusing the Grid: Variations on a Square Theme). Wendy seemed to like it and I had no idea what she would do with it. Sadly, we don't have a photograph of this exact block prior to the exchange, but you can see what it was like in a similar photograph (at right).

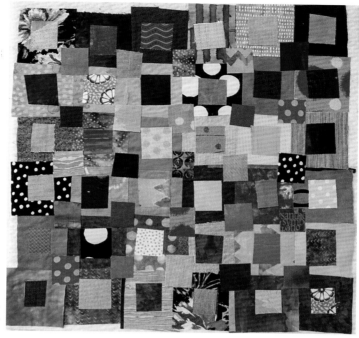

A fused block similar to the one I gave Wendy

Round 2:
Wendy Satin Stitches

I got back my piece with some of the most wonderful satin stitching I have ever seen. Wendy likes things neat, so she covered up all the raw edges of my fused squares. In addition, she also gave me an 18″ × 18″ quilt top with taupe fabric. Wendy had satin stitched around invisible blocks using the same colors of thread.

Round 3:
Pat Fuses Again

I decided to add more fused smaller bits of dotty fabrics to my original fused piece. The taupe piece of fabric with satin stitching around invisible blocks was another story—I wanted this piece to have a more textured, free-form feel about it, so I fused some small pieces of fabric onto it and stitched pieces of tulle and organza on top.

I had no idea how these two pieces would go together, but I knew two was an even number, not good in the design world. Clearly, we needed one more piece in this mix, so I gave Wendy an 18″ × 18″ piece of home dec–weight linen ikat with colorful woven squares against a cream background. Repeating the square theme seemed like a great idea to me. I also fused small squares of fabric onto this piece, but they didn't stay there for long.

Round 4: Back to Wendy

Wendy ripped those carefully fused pieces of fabric off of the ikat panel (with a smile on her face, I'm sure). She had a different idea, and it turned out great. She loved the way the fibers brushed out along the edges of the squares in the woven panel and thought she could emphasize this effect. Wendy layered two squares of frayed shot cotton over every woven square, so the stacked squares are small, medium, and large. She quilted a grid using an altered straight stitch (see Thread Texturing, Surface Stitching, and Satin-Stitched Triangles, page 100) to add even more texture.

Photo by Wendy Hill

Round 5: Not Too Messy for Pat

The taupe piece came back pretty much as I had handed it over to Wendy. She said she'd have a panic attack if she had to fuse fabrics with abandon. So I added more fused pieces to the taupe square. Then I decided to do some additional quilting within the blocks using a taupe thread.

Finishing the Quilt

We decided to keep the squares in three separate pieces rather than do any more cutting or sewing to integrate them. We planned to hang them together as a triptych. They are all approximately 18″ × 18″ square. I said they were close enough and Wendy agreed (and resisted the urge to square them up to the same size).

Instead of finishing the pieces with binding or a facing, we decided to finish the outside edges with satin stitching (see Professional-Looking Satin-Stitched Edge Finish, page 99). Wendy used the same Sulky Blendables variegated thread on all three pieces, which helps pull these different squares together.

Why It Works

Square Dance is all about repetition. Squares are dancing all over the place, on top of each other and beneath. The three sections each measure about 18″ × 18″ square, and each contains a basic yet distinct grid pattern. Squares are fused, stitched, cut out, and woven into the fabric. Each is a unique piece, but they all dance together nicely.

Our final decision was how to hang *Square Dance*. We think it looks best when viewed vertically, with the busiest section at the top. As the eye travels down to the next two sections, a transition occurs: From complex to minimal, the squares disintegrate before your eyes.

The Collection

About This Challenge

Around 2007, we independently started collecting Echino fabrics, designed by Etsuko Furuya for Kokka (a Japanese manufacturer known for graphic, modern, trendy styles by several designers). Over the years, other designers and fabric companies started producing similar home decor–weight cotton, cotton/linen blends, and linen fabrics.

These fabrics just get better after washing. We've used these fabrics in pillows, tote bags, and of course, quilts.

When we became aware of our mutual love for these fabrics, it accelerated our collecting. While traveling, we shared images of new fabrics over our phones, scooping up ones we didn't already have. Of course we centered a challenge around our contemporary Japanese fabrics. We kept our rules simple: primarily use the imported fabrics from Japan. For your Collection challenge, consider the following ideas:

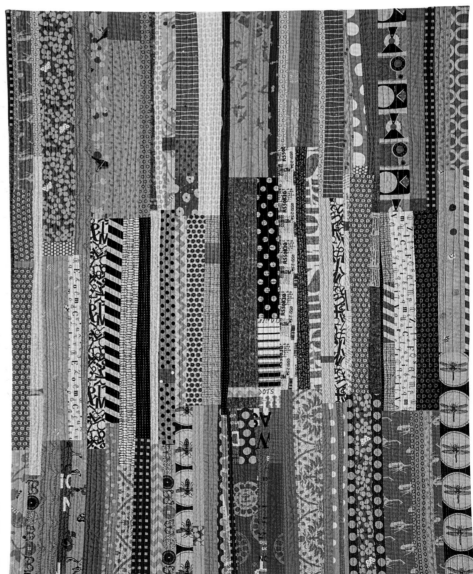

Echino Yet Again
by Pat Pease,
40½″ × 52″

Pat uses her collection of Echino fabrics.

MAKE IT YOUR OWN

Think about the following:

- Use a particular style of fabric such as big florals, novelty prints, stripes, reproduction fabrics, and so on.

- Use a collection based on a predetermined color scheme.

- Divide a shared collection of assorted fabrics among all the participants.

- Go beyond a fabric collection to include techniques and other "ingredients."

Ripple Effect
by Wendy Hill,
41¾" × 30½"

Wendy uses her collection of
contemporary Japanese fabric.

PAT'S QUILT:
Echino Yet Again

USING A COLLECTION OF ECHINO FABRICS …

Echino Yet Again
by Pat Pease,
40½" × 52"

In the Beginning

Five years ago I made a quilt out of mostly Echino fabrics, and I called it *Put a Bird on It* (page 110). Sometimes it spends time on a guest bed, or else in a closet. It is a "no dogs allowed" quilt, though several have been caught sleeping on it.

I have continued to collect Japanese fabrics, and as my small stacks of them grew higher and higher, it was clearly time to do something with them.

Photo by Gary Alvis

Detail of *Put a Bird on It* (page 110)

Color and Design Decisions

I spent the better part of a day sorting my fabrics by color and then by value within the color families. Because many of these fabrics are multicolored, I had to determine what the main color was. This is a fun exercise, and it can really help you to develop an eye for color as well as value. Try it, then check what you have done using the plastic value finders in the Ultimate 3-in-1 Color Tool (by C&T Publishing; see Resources, page 111) or by photographing or photocopying them in black and white. You might be surprised by the results.

Colors First

I already knew I was going to use mostly Japanese fabrics—my next decision was to come up with a color scheme. My first Echino quilt used just about every color you can think of. This time I wanted to make a quilt that was more controlled, so I decided on a triadic color scheme—a scheme that uses three colors equidistant from each other on the color wheel. The collection includes both Japanese and other fabrics.

Triadic color scheme—blue-green, red-violet, and yellow-orange

Black-and-White Fabrics Next

In addition, I decided to use some of the black-and-white print fabrics I have. These fabrics have a wide range of scale of the print and value from light to dark, though dots, letters, and numbers appear on most. In other words, there was a lot of variety, but it was controlled rather than chaotic.

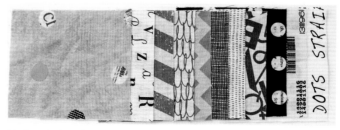

Black-and-white fabrics

Under Construction

Unit construction was simple. I started out cutting long strips of fabric with just my rotary cutter (no ruler). I wanted the strips to be uneven to make them interesting and to give the quilt movement, rather than the static look you get when all the strips are cut exactly the same. Uneven lines give you different paths to follow and surprises when they abruptly end.

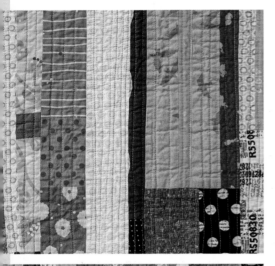

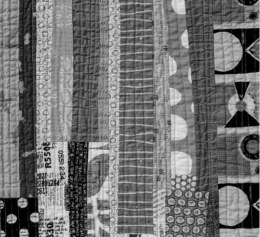

TIP

Adding Movement with Free-Form Cutting

To get fabric units that are not straight is really not that difficult and adds great movement to a quilt. Cut two strips of fabric without using a ruler, allowing a generous seam allowance. When you sew the strips together, ignore the urge to use a precise ¼"—Wendy and I both use wide seam allowances, sometimes up to ½", so when piecing this way, we have more latitude. Press the seams open. You can also force a seam to be crooked by ironing, not pressing it. Try making a few more units to get your desired look.

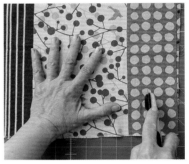

Free-form cutting a strip of fabric

After I sewed strips into workable units, I auditioned them on my design wall in a horizontal format. Some of the fabric prints were so lovely I hated to cut them up, but then, why did I have them? To help the whites, grays, and blacks look more unified within the quilt, I sewed a small strip of color into it before I made the unit. And fortunately, some of the gray fabric had spots of blue-green and yellow-orange, further helping to tie the piece together as the colors flow across from one highly colored area to the other.

Detail of colored strip sewn into black-and-white fabric

I sewed more and more units together until I had reached a size I was happy with. All the units were up on my design wall, but something was terribly wrong.

Point of View

This is why it is so important to step back and look at your work as you proceed. It is much easier to change blocks, units, or pieces before you get too far. At first I thought the color scheme might be the problem, because I had pushed my selected colors to the neighboring colors on the color wheel. Borrowing from neighboring colors can be a really good thing (see Wendy's Color Neighborhood, page 15) and I was happy with the way the colors and the values played together. I had lots of different sizes of prints and an interesting mix of black, white, and gray fabric. So the color scheme was good.

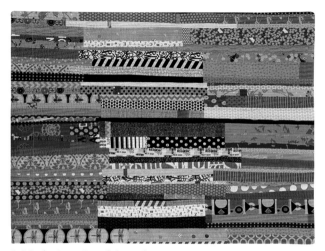

Original orientation of the quilt

I turned the quilt upside down to see if that would help, but it didn't. Then I tried it vertically (see Finding the Right Orientation, page 17) and I was amazed. I had one of those *Aha!* moments. Turning it made everything fall into place. I had the orientation of the quilt wrong, and that was an easy fix. Now this may be totally personal, but for me, it made all the difference in the world because it reinforces the vertical nature of the strips.

Quilting

As is usual for me, I used heavyweight thread so the quilting lines would be obvious. I picked thread colors that repeated the colors of the fabric, such as bright orange, aqua blue, lavender, and purple. These colorful stitching lines help to unify the quilt.

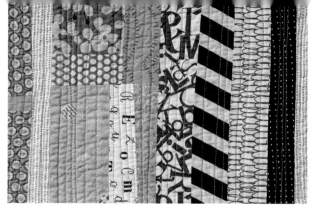

Quilting lines from the front

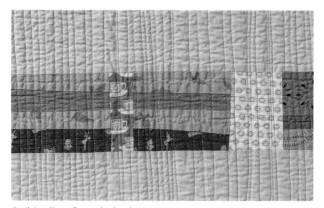

Quilting lines from the back

Why It Works

Echino Yet Again is one of my favorite quilts. Yes, it is simple, but there can be beauty in simplicity. Vertical strips cut free-form repeat the vertical orientation of the quilt. This form is also repeated in the bright, heavy stitching lines. I love the fabrics I used and think there isn't a single one that doesn't belong. Also, the interesting fabric choices draw the viewer in. What quilt doesn't need transistor radios, helicopters, and dragonflies? Also, the colorful stitching lines help unify the top of the quilt with the bottom. Your eye keeps moving around the quilt to see what else is there.

The black, white, and gray fabrics are full of interesting details. There are small and large dots, along with numerous strips that have letters and numbers. These types of details help to draw the eye of the viewer in to see what they are, and perhaps what they say. They also add a lot of visual texture to an otherwise simple quilt.

In addition to its strong vertical look, there are lots of dots and circular shapes in this quilt. They vary in size and color. Even the dragonflies have large circles around them. A repeated shape is always a unifying factor.

WENDY'S QUILT:
Ripple Effect

USING A COLLECTION OF CONTEMPORARY JAPANESE FABRICS ...

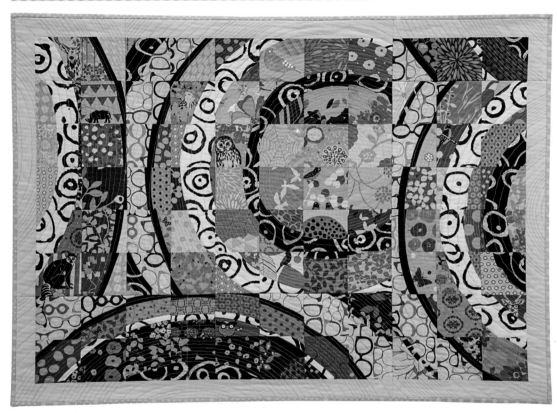

Ripple Effect
by Wendy Hill,
41¾" × 30½"

In the Beginning

Almost fifteen years ago, I became obsessed with circles, arcs, and related wavy-line patterns. And I still look for new ways to play with these patterns. For this quilt, an aerial photograph of concentric rings in the sand brought other similar images to mind, such as drops of water in a puddle, or raindrops on a flat lake. I had to follow the idea of ripples.

My initial full-size drawing of concentric circles with complicated overlapping and mirror imaging went nowhere fast. Without much thinking, I cut up, rearranged, and altered the drawing, and knew I was onto something!

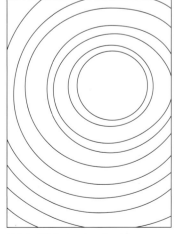

Original full-size drawing of concentric circles

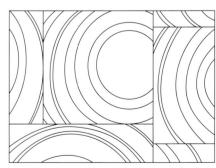

Same full-size drawing cut up, reassembled, and altered

Color and Design Decisions

I tend to make things more complicated than they need to be, so it's no surprise that I tripped over myself with this quilt, too. I started auditioning fabrics, but a few days later I could see it was a big muddled mess. I kept thinking I could force things to work, but these rigid thoughts prevented me from problem solving and thinking creatively.

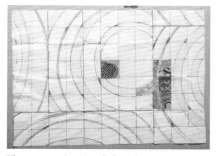

The narrow rings in a light value did not work.

Up close the arcs had good definition, but from a few feet away it all blended together.

Photo by Wendy Hill

After I let it all go, new ideas flooded my mind. Pat encouraged me to group similar colors in the arcs, and she donated fabrics to widen my color choices (thanks, Pat). Coincidentally, three new fabric purchases turned out to be just right for the new direction. The colors quickly emerged: oranges, blues, greens, and violets (which incidentally turns out to be very close to a double split-complementary color scheme) plus mottled hand-dyed black batik, a sunglasses print, a white print on black, and the reverse black print on white.

TIP

Using Color Families

Notice how the color groupings spill over into other related color families. I call it "going next door or across the street," referring to my color neighborhood concept (see Wendy's Color Neighborhood, page 15). For example, the oranges range from pink-orange to tangerine, red-orange, burnt orange, and oxblood. The same wide mix is seen with the other color families. If you think oxblood is an odd choice, with roots in the red color family, cover up the oxblood-brown arc at the bottom of the quilt: This is the color that brings all the others into sharp focus.

Under Construction

All the arcs line up in the life-size drawing, but I wanted just the opposite. I kept seeing ripples bumping up against each other in my mind. The curved lines had to be disrupted.

Freezer-Paper Patterns

I traced freezer-paper patterns for each of the 88 units. A little time spent numbering the patterns and sorting the units by row saved plenty of time later when auditioning the fabrics in small areas or clusters.

Original freezer-paper templates

Planning Ahead

I added a seam allowance between the pieces inside the unit but not on the outside edges. Also, I did not sew consistently even seam allowances. Remember, I did *not* want the curved lines to line up smoothly. With no added seam allowance around the outside edge, the *bite* of my wider seam allowance let the curved lines *jog* a little bit.

Notice the freehand-cut seam allowances on the arcs but not on the straight outside edges.

The unit is approximately 4¼" square before squaring-up to 4".

Fussy Cutting

I had put a ring-tailed lemur front and center in my original-and-then-abandoned layout. This would have been great in a quilt for a baby or child, but not so great for my idea. Instead, I fussy cut animals and other motifs so they were off center, slightly hidden, or missing a body part. I kept the fun of these fabrics while letting viewers discover these elements on closer viewing.

Quilting-as-You-Sew with Batting

I planned to echo quilt (see Echo Quilting with a Walking Foot, page 70) a mildly wavy line following the arcs of each of the five ripples. If I had attempted this after the entire quilt top had been pieced, I would have had hundreds of thread tails to deal with while handling a much larger quilt. Instead, I echo quilted each of the five sections, basted to batting only (see Quilting-as-You-Sew to Batting, page 97). All thread tails were now in the seam allowances. And as a bonus, it was much easier to quilt the smaller sections rather than the whole quilt.

After quilting, I sewed the sections right sides together, layered the quilted top with the backing, and added enough quilting to hold the layers together. In this case, all I needed was to stitch-in-the-ditch.

Quilting-in-the-ditch through all the layers is enough for this small wall quilt.

Why It Works

Everything works together to achieve the desired overall effect of ripples pushing against each other, in motion even as the viewer looks at the quilt. The Japanese contemporary fabrics can lean toward the cute side, but the offset fussy cutting with the jostling curved lines to create the arcs gives this quilt a sophisticated look. Because the fabrics are grouped in the partial circles and arcs, the colors and values work together to let the viewer clearly see the pattern of the ripples.

The two color families, oranges and blues, and greens and violets, are almost opposites on the color wheel. This complementary (or double split-complementary, depending upon your interpretation) color scheme provides contrast and contributes to the illusion of the ripples pushing against each other. But I did not stick to rigid textbook definitions when choosing colors and fabrics. A lot of the colors are cousins from close color family relatives.

Repetition of the circular motif is everywhere in this composition: the five ripple patterns, the motifs in the fabrics, the quilting lines that echo the arcs, and so on.

The eye is drawn to the focal point—the largest partial circle just off-center and to the right. From there, the eye follows various ripples pushing against each other, back to the focal point. Around and around you go, finding something new to look at each time.

6

Invent Your Own Challenge

About This Challenge

Every time you decide to make a quilt, you are in a sense inventing your own challenge. However, we often stay within familiar territory, whether it is colors, fabric styles, quilt patterns, or techniques. With this type of open-ended challenge, you can explore just about anything you want, in any size, with any techniques and any materials.

Wendy chose the theme "Keep It Simple," for the simple reason that she complicates every single idea she has. Pat decided to challenge herself to sew inset circles. Pat jokes she doesn't actually know how to sew. Without planning it, we each challenged ourselves to address our perceived weak areas.

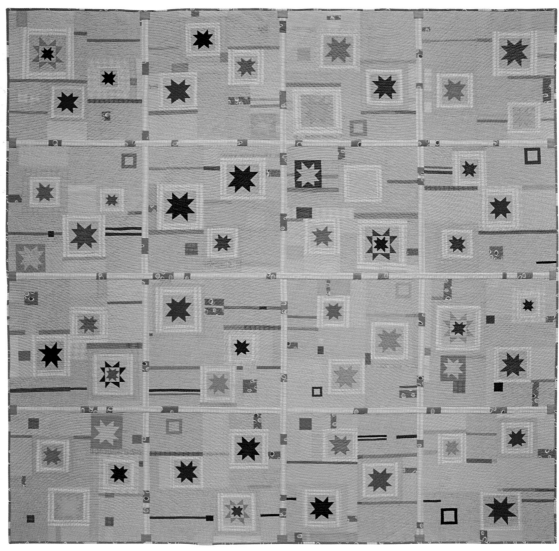

Color Blinded Again (Side 2 of *ColorBlind*)
by Wendy Hill,
92″ × 92″

Wendy tries to keep it simple.

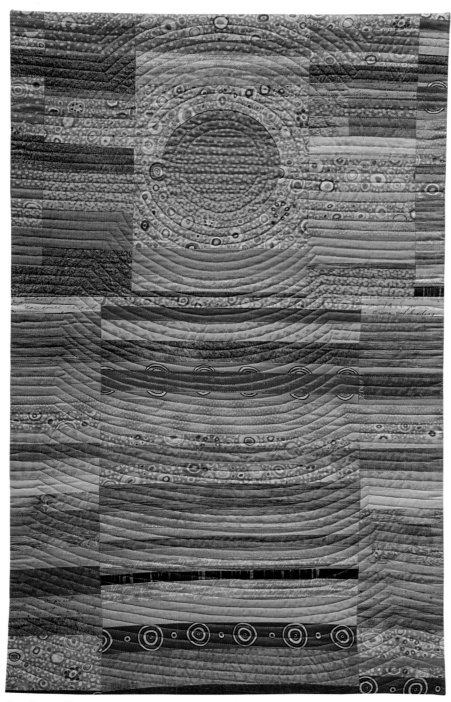

MAKE IT YOUR OWN

Go for it with these ideas:

- Evaluate your habits. Choose something new to try.

- Review your wish list of quilt ideas and choose one that has stumped you.

- Look at a UFO (unfinished object) that has been cast aside. Salvage the quilt through a process of examining what is working and not working, and finish it. If the quilt can't be saved, transform it into something useful, such as a dog bed, pillow, purse, or something else.

One Orange Dot
by Pat Pease,
20½″ × 32½″

Pat tries a new technique: inset circles.

WENDY'S QUILT:
Color Blinded Again

KEEPING IT SIMPLE …

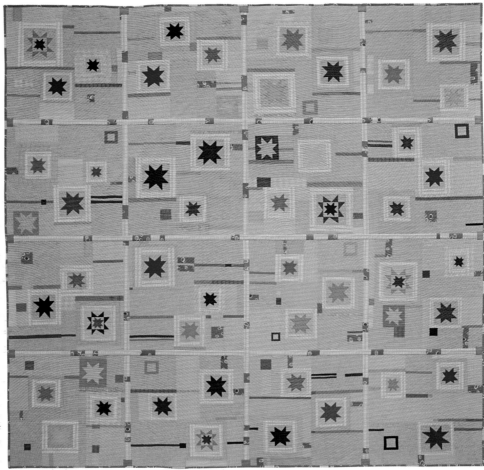

Color Blinded Again
by Wendy Hill,
92″ × 92″

This quilt is the
reverse side of
ColorBlind
(page 18).

In the Beginning

At first, it may look like I once again complicated what should have been a simple quilt. But don't let the size fool you into thinking it is complicated. While working on the Value of Value challenge (page 18), I asked myself a series of "what if" questions about the opposite of all that chaos and riot of color. Through a process of sketching and notes, I answered it—free-form Sawtooth Stars floating against a sea of neutral. I was still making the blocks for *ColorBlind* (page 18), so I decided it would be fun to make the quilt reversible: literally and figuratively opposites of each other! I told myself I would get two quilts in the time it takes to make one (which is, of course, delusional), but it is fun to be surprised by the flip side.

TIP

Planning Ahead

Planning ahead is required for making reversible quilts, but as with any quilt, there will be forks in the road (decisions), dead ends (unforeseen problems), and possibly a crash in the ditch (an actual mistake). This cycle of trial and evaluation is at the heart of the creative process.

Color and Design Decisions

The limited palette, with a neutral background and solid-color stars, could have resulted in something static, with no life at all. To avoid that, I did two things:

- I used a wide assortment of neutral fabrics in a variety of visual and physical textures that blend together into a unified background—a sea of neutrals. This subtle effect helps create the mood and the illusion that the stars are

advancing and receding against the background. In this case, *more is less* creates a cohesive, interesting neutral background. With only one neutral fabric, less certainly would not have resulted in more.

- I chose solid fabrics that aren't solid—assorted shot cottons—for the stars because of the way they are woven. The final color is the result of one color in the warp and a different color in the weft. The new, blended color radiates a depth not possible with true solid colors, which have the same color warp and weft. Shot cottons give more bang for the fabric-choice buck. I selected 50 different lights, mediums, and darks from just about every color family for the 50 free-form-pieced Sawtooth Stars.

TIP

Using "Shot" Fabrics

Many types of fabrics are made with two colors, one in the warp and a different color in the weft, not just cottons. Look for shot silks, linens, rayons, and blends. When one color is white, the fabric is often called *chambray*.

Row 1: Polished shot cottons and chambrays. *Row 2:* Shot cottons with a lower thread count / thicker yarn. *Row 3:* Shot cottons with a higher thread count / thinner yarn. *Row 4:* Dupioni shot silks. *Row 5:* Shot silks and silk/rayon blends.

Color Conversations

Colors and values are always fluid. Both work together to create mood and evoke feelings. By observing what happens when colors meet, you can almost hear a color conversation going on. Experiment with fabric combinations to find the conversation that is right for your project. When color and design come together, your quilts can speak for you.

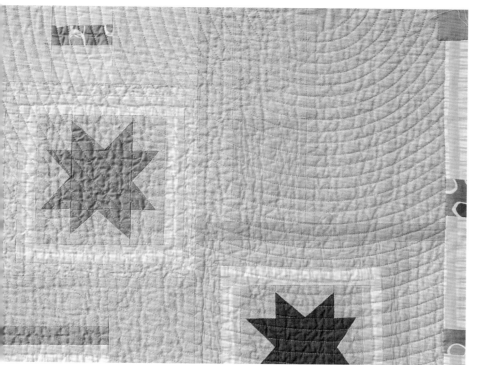

Under Construction

I knew I had to make a lot of free-form Sawtooth Stars and gather as many neutral fabrics as I could to start work on this side of the reversible quilt. I had a lot of work to do!

Free-Form Sawtooth Stars

Sawtooth Stars are drafted on an unequal nine-patch grid. The center square is twice the height of the outside squares and rectangles.

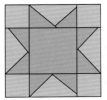

Free-form Sawtooth Star

When making free-form Sawtooth Stars (see Free-Form Sawtooth Stars, page 90), this basic relationship is loosely retained but the star points are randomly shaped. I constructed approximately 50 small, medium, and large star blocks in different shot cotton colors.

Making Quilts Reversible

For me, solving problems is always a motivation to use different methods or techniques. For this quilt, the size (92″ × 92″) was my biggest problem. I decided to break the quilt down into 16 sections, using one of my quilting-as-you-sew methods (pages 95 and 97).

1. I pieced the 64 blocks for Side 1 (*ColorBlind*) into 16 blocks, each with 4 squares almost 25″ × 25″.

2. For Side 2 (*Color Blinded Again*), I designed and pieced 16 big blocks, each about 26″ × 26″. Using big sheets of newsprint, I auditioned and pinned the approximately 50 free-form Sawtooth Stars ahead of time. I added the neutral background around the stars, piecing everything together to make the mini-quilt tops.

3. I layered, basted, and quilted the 16 panels, treating them like 16 small quilts. Each small "quilt" had a Side 1 panel, batting, and a Side 2 panel. Advance planning is required to make sure all the pieced blocks on Side 1 and the big blocks on Side 2 remain in the correct order and orientation at the end.

4. I echo quilted the 16 basted panels from Side 2, using a walking foot and a freezer-paper template to get the curved lines started (see Echo Quilting with a Walking Foot, page 70). I washed, dried, and squared-up the panels before proceeding.

5. I assembled the final quilt in 4 rows, with each row consisting of 4 big blocks. With the Side 1 panels sewn right sides together, this side looks like any other quilt. I covered the seams on Side 2 with self-made fabric seam covers (see Quilting-As-You-Go with Seam Covers, page 95). The seam covers on Side 2 look like sashing.

BASTING

As a self-taught quilter from a long time ago, I never learned to use safety pins to baste a quilt. I taught myself to hand baste the quilt sandwich using basting thread (thread made specifically for basting that is fine and breaks rather than tearing the fabric when you pull it out) with large stitches, 3″–4″ long.

I still hand baste when the situation calls for it, but several years ago I added spray basting and machine basting with water-soluble thread to my bag of tricks. The combination of spray basting and a machine-stitched grid (about 3″–4″ apart) securely holds the quilt sandwich together in a way that safety pins can't. You'll have unlimited freedom to handle the quilt.

There is variety in the size of the stars, ranging from small to large, with a few outliers in both directions.

Finding Goldilocks: Balance, Unity, Variety

Variety keeps the composition interesting. If there is too much variety, though, chaos can ensue—when there is no place for the eye to rest, the viewer can't take it all in.

But when there is too much uniformity, the viewer can understand the entire image with a glance, and it's boring. It's the interplay of balance, unity, and variety that creates enough tension and movement to keep the viewer engaged without being overwhelmed.

I tried to find that balance between boredom and insanity, where the viewer would never get tired of looking at the quilt. Here are some examples of choices I made:

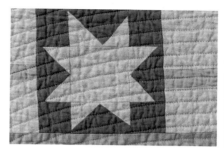
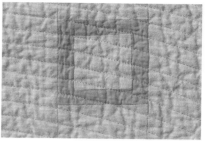

"Inside out" stars and squares repeat the star and square motifs in a surprising way.

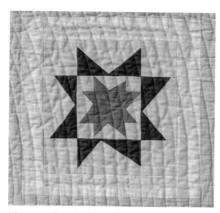
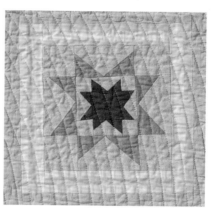

There are five double stars sprinkled through the composition.

Every star is outlined with this gray-and-white fabric.

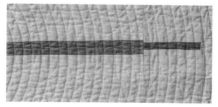

A variety of horizontal lines in neutrals and colors break up the sea of neutrals and lead the eye around the composition.

The nine orange rectangles at the ends of the sashing lines help pull the whole composition together. Cover up the rectangles with your finger to see how their absence changes everything.

Why It Works

There is an illusion of depth and movement for something so simple: multi-colored stars against a neutral background. Careful consideration of fabric choices, variety in size and scale of the stars and horizontal lines, surprise elements such as the "inside out" stars and squares, repetition of the star motif with the double stars, and all of the other choices lend a playfulness to the composition. The viewer can see a pattern of stars without the composition's being too chaotic or too uniform. I took a gamble when making this quilt so large because it could have been a great big bore. But I felt it needed to be this large to create the mood and evoke the feelings I imagined.

PAT'S QUILT:
One Orange Dot

FOCUSING ON CIRCLES ...

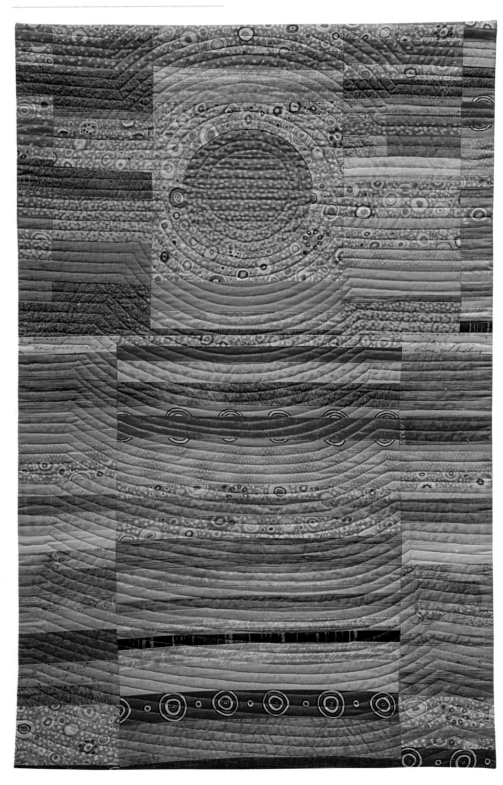

One Orange Dot
by Pat Pease,
20½″ × 32½″

In the Beginning

I've had a love affair with polka dots for a very long time. Large or small, subtle or in-your-face obvious, their energy and playfulness make me smile. Polka dots seem to find a way into almost every quilt I make, often to liven things up or as a repeated design element. Several years ago I took a class from Dale Fleming based on her book *Pieced Curves So Simple: The 6-Minute Circle and Other Time-Saving Delights*. I imagined future quilts scattered with large and small perfect circles, but that

was not to be. It soon became clear to me that I was far from being a natural with the 6-Minute Circle as others around me turned out lovely circles of all sizes in record time.

The 6-Minute Circle in progress

Unfortunately, I had to leave the workshop early, and the thought of being a 6-Minute Circle master fled from my mind. I decided to let the fabric I printed and purchased bring the circles to my quilts.

Color and Design Decisions

When I was thinking about ideas for my personal challenge quilt, my mind drifted back to those circles I had tried to make years ago. I decided to try it one more time, and my quilt *One Orange Dot* is the result of this effort. This 6-Minute Circle seemed like it took me six hours to complete, but it was done, and I was oh so happy. I originally planned to make more circles, but I figured it would be better to leave well enough alone. My one orange circle took center stage on my design wall. I found some yellow and orange fabric that I thought might work well with it, and they were soon on my design wall as well.

Fabric Experimentation

A quick check with my Ultimate 3-in-1 Color Tool (by C&T Publishing; see Resources, page 111) let me know I was headed in the right direction. An analogous golden-yellow, orange-yellow, and yellow-orange combination would work. There are more than 30 different fabrics in *One Orange Dot*, and a good number came from my scraps. I save most of my scraps, including small ones that most

quilters would probably toss out. Sometimes these small pieces can add just that spark or subtle value change that livens up a quilt. All of my scraps are sorted by color in large colored plastic tubs that I keep underneath my cutting table. This is an easy way for me to keep scraps under control yet still have easy access to them. As I dug through the yellow and orange tubs, I found some treasures that were soon up on my design wall.

Tubs of scraps

AUDITIONING FABRIC

Auditioning fabric is my favorite part of making a quilt. The big surprise is when I find something I bought years ago that is just perfect for the quilt I am making today. Sometimes I find small pieces in my scrap tubs that are different values than what I am looking for, and I always try those out; they might just be perfect. Don't be afraid to try out different patterns, be they subtle or bold. And be sure to think about what the fabric will look like when it is cut up into smaller pieces. Wendy has shown me on more than one occasion that bold or busy fabric can look totally different when it is cut up.

The Ultimate 3-in-1 Color Tool helps make color choices easy and virtually foolproof. I find that when I'm working on a quilt and there seems to be something wrong with the color, the Color Tool can be a lifesaver. It helps me select the right tints (color + white), shades (color + black), and tones (color + gray) of the fabric colors I'm working with. Quilts that have just a few pieces of the same fabric colors can sometimes look flat or almost lifeless. Adding pieces of many different fabrics in a range of one color can add a certain sparkle or lifelike quality to a quilt. The eye moves around to different areas of interest.

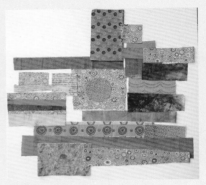

Auditioning fabric on the design wall

Under Construction

After a few quick sketches, I had a plan, and knew I wanted to proceed with a string-pieced quilt with my one orange dot as the focal point. I cut strips of fabric, sometimes using a ruler and sometimes not. I sewed the strips into units using a healthy ½˝ seam allowance and pressed the seams open. After sewing a number of units together, I auditioned them on my design wall, and I continued with this process until I was pleased with the composition. Sometimes these units were sliced in two, with more fabric added in the middle. If it worked, it stayed. If it didn't, it might be cut into smaller units, go into the scrap tubs, be added later, or even turn up in another quilt. I layered the quilt with batting and a backing fabric, and then finally quilted it on my sewing machine with a walking foot.

TIP

- -

Big Seam Allowances

I like to use a big seam allowance when piecing, and I press my seams open. Sometimes my seam allowance can be up to ½″, which I know seems huge. I put all kinds of fabrics in my quilts, including some most people don't use. I've included linen, silks of all kinds and weights, canvas, tulle, wool, acid-free paper, hemp, and whatever else I think will work. Pressing my seams open makes my quilts flatter, and a larger seam allowance is easier to press open.

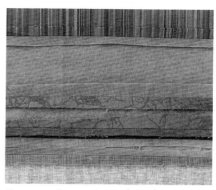

Generous ½″ seam allowances pressed open

- -

Why It Works

The Importance of Repetition

The focal point of this quilt is clearly the one orange dot. To add visual weight to the dot, I deliberately positioned the print with the denser clusters of dots at the bottom of the circle.

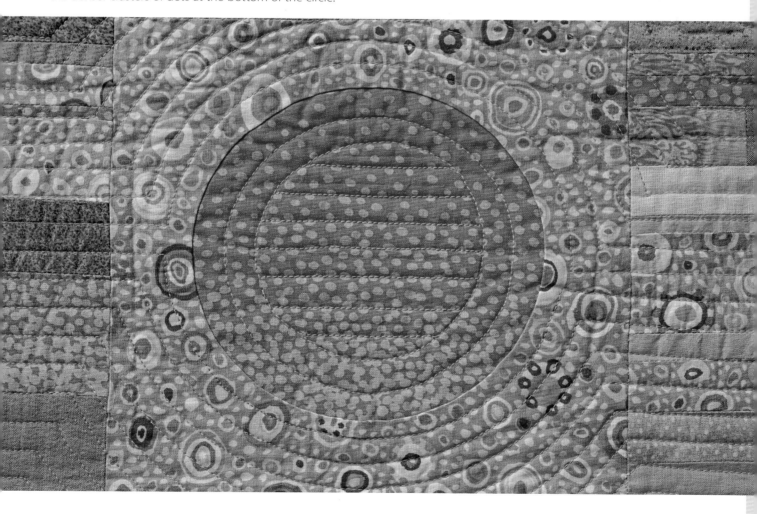

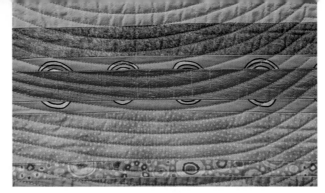

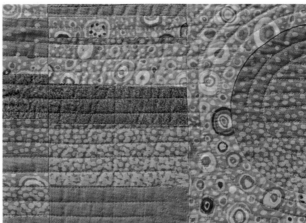

I used nine fabrics with circle motifs, which vary in color and scale. I selected these fabrics to repeat the shape of the orange dot. Some of the fabrics are so subtle in their pattern that the dots are barely noticeable, yet they play an integral part in the quilt. As you get closer to the quilt, they become more obvious and help move the eye around the quilt.

Even the quilting echoes the circle patterns while straight lines repeat the lines in the string piecing. I used the walking foot on my machine to follow the dot, and then pivoted to follow the strings. The 30-weight cotton thread makes the quilting lines stand out. Straight lines fill in the center of the one orange dot.

ECHO QUILTING WITH A WALKING FOOT

Echo quilting with the feed dogs up is an easy way to add curved quilting lines. We generally follow the edge of a template (*ColorBlind*, page 18 / *Color Blinded Again*, page 60) or a shape in the quilt (*Ripple Effect*, page 51, and *One Orange Dot*, page 61), but not always. Judge the distance by eye or line up the edge of the walking foot to follow the original shape and subsequent stitching lines. Move the sewing machine needle left or right to adjust the width of the echo quilting lines.

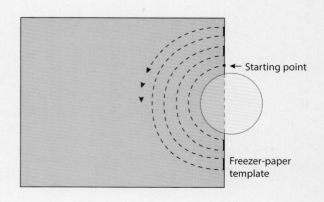

← Starting point

Freezer-paper template

Balancing Act

All of the fabric choices I made during construction were very intentional. I used commercial cottons, shot cotton, silk, and raw silk, each with its own properties. Some of the silks and cottons are shiny, others dull or matte, and the raw silk has an almost fuzzy texture. I used pure colors, but rust, brown, and gold push the boundaries of my original color scheme of golden yellow to yellow-orange. I even borrowed from the red-orange color family by including a deep shade of orange that is almost mahogany. There isn't a lot of that mahogany, but just enough. If you look closely, you will see that some of the gold and orange fabrics have a lavender wash that dulls them just a bit. That lavender hints at the lavender circles in the fabric that surround the orange dot. Even the red-orange linen has subtle stripes of gold in it, to tie it in with the other golden fabrics.

Orange fabric with lavender and gold wash

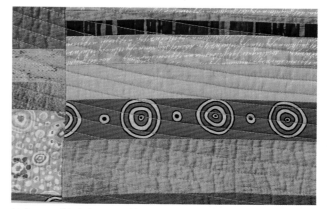

Mahogany fabric borrowed from red-orange family

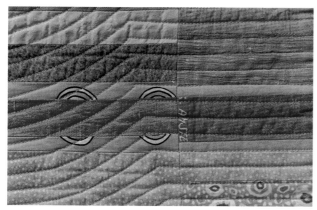

Assorted fabrics around the orange family of colors

Lots of Lines

All the strings that surround the orange circle are lines of color. Some are muted and others are bold and obvious. The darker colors command your attention, and the muted ones seem to recede. Some are more than 2″ tall, while others are less than ¼″. With string piecing you can continue a line across the quilt or chop it up into segments. I chose to vary the length of the strings to add visual interest and make the eye jump from one line to the next. The only continuous lines in the piece are the quilting lines.

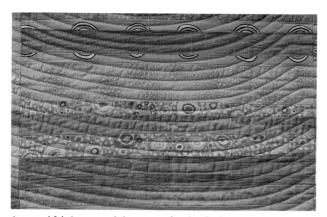

Silk fabric detail

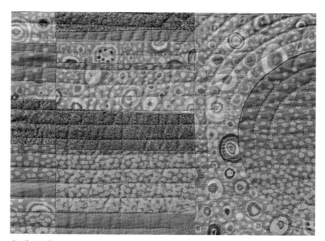

Quilting lines

7

Mix It Up

About This Challenge

This last challenge is the most open-ended of all: Mix It Up.

As with many quilters, we share the dilemma of having too many ideas and not enough time. It's no wonder that we stick to what we know best. So we wanted to design a challenge that would allow us to focus on mixing it up: trying something new to go along with what we know best. We talked about surface manipulation, painting, printing, stamping, and the like. We didn't get to throw in everything we wanted to try (that would be way too much), but this challenge sent both of us in new directions and we were very happy with the results.

Wendy wanted to go back to her roots with surface stitching and making "new" fabrics while pushing herself to use the techniques she has learned about thread texturing and quilting since the early 1990s. Pat decided to try painting and stamping, and after a bit of trial and error, decided on a combination of the two, along with a new (to her) technique for assembling a quilt.

Cut Up
by Pat Pease,
24½″ × 24½″

Pat tries painting and stamping along with using a new (to her) technique— raw-edge construction.

MAKE IT YOUR OWN

When shaping your own Mix It Up challenge, consider these ideas:

- Use mixed-media techniques: more than one medium in the quilt, such as fabric painting and dyeing; thread embellishment; collage; textured fabric with paint, pastels, gel medium; paper or other nonfabric materials; embellishments; and so on.

- Focus on one or two new techniques or materials, combining them with your familiar processes.

- Share the same mixing-it-up ideas among all the participants, or let individuals design their own mix.

Confluence
by Wendy Hill,
30″ × 19″

Wendy uses surface stitching and making "new" fabrics (an old standby for her) while pushing herself with everything she's learned about thread texturing and quilting since the early 1990s.

PAT'S QUILT: *Cut Up*

PAINTING, STAMPING,
AND RAW-EDGE
CONSTRUCTION ...

Cut Up
by Pat Pease,
24½" × 24½"

In the Beginning

Cut Up started out as a riot of colorful free-form blocks. I sewed blocks at a rapid pace, using mostly bright, contemporary Japanese fabrics. Surrounded by piles of fabric, I made more and more blocks of varying sizes and colors.

Meanwhile, I took occasional breaks from sewing to experiment with some paints and stencils I had, and found I got the best results with Tim Holtz Distress Paint (see Resources, page 111). This acid-free acrylic paint comes in 1 fluid ounce bottles that have dabbers at the top that make perfectly shaped dots. The fine print on the label says it can be used on multiple surfaces, so I tried it on fabric. The paint dried a bit stiff, but since I was making a wall quilt, it really didn't concern me. I could make all the polka dots I wanted and was limited only by the colors of paint or fabric that I had.

Stamped fabric

TIP

Painting Fabric

I used Distress Paint to make my own dotted fabric. I find it best to work on a padded surface and apply medium pressure. When you are finished making the marks you want, just twist off the cover of the bottle and run the dabber under cool water. It will be ready to go the next time you want to paint.

Color and Design Decisions

Too Much of a Good Thing

I put 37 blocks on my design wall and realized I might not be on the right track. All the bright-colored polka-dotted and striped blocks were having a fight with each other right before my eyes. I had overdone it. Additionally, one block clearly did not belong. It was dark and almost sorry looking, compared with the riot of color I saw before me.

Blocks on the wall

I tried to rearrange the blocks and eliminated some. The only solution I came up with was to surround each block with a lot of neutral fabric, but that was not what I had planned. These blocks belonged in another quilt. Then my eyes went back to that dark, moody block. I really liked it.

Choosing Fabrics and Colors

Wendy and I had once talked about using a fabric print as a focus fabric—taking all the colors from that piece of fabric and using them as the color scheme without actually using the focus fabric in the quilt. This seemed like such a good idea at the time, and this was the perfect time to try it out for myself. I would use the colors from a fabric I had used to make that dark, moody block.

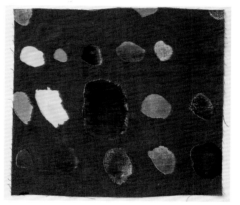

Nani Iro two-ply double gauze dots in a dark aqua green

I found fabrics that matched and almost matched the colors within the dark green fabric. Really bright colors were just too much of a contrast, so I selected mostly muted shades. Purples ranged from inky dark to mid-range. I found a few dark blues and acidy yellows and greens. Silk, burlap, hand-dyed cottons from Africa, shot cottons, commercial cottons, and gauze were all in the mix. However, I still went back to the original piece of dark green fabric (the focus fabric) and decided to include it after all. I knew it would be somewhat difficult to work with, but I couldn't leave it out.

Fabric choices

Under Construction

I took a free-form approach to putting together the blocks. Most have three or four fabric strips sewn together, while others have a few more. *Cut Up* is another string quilt using blocks as the unit of construction. I layered a few strips on top of some blocks, and aimed for a block that was about 4″–5″ square. After I finished sewing the blocks, I trimmed them to about 4″ × 4″ and then arranged them on my design wall.

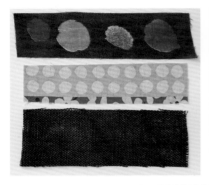 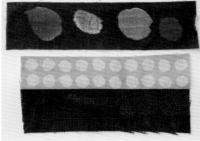 

Texture Decisions

Because I used burlap, hemp, and two-ply gauze along with cottons and silks, I had some construction issues. Some of the blocks were thin, others thick, and some were both. Sewing them all together nicely would be a challenge in itself. In addition to the thickness issue, many of the fabrics had started to ravel; rather than be bothered by this, I embraced it.

Look for vendors or stores that sell specialty fabrics, such as Fiber on a Whim or Seed to Sewer (see Resources, page 111).

Raw-Edge Construction

I love the look of fraying fabric, so I decided to use Sulky KK 2000 Temporary Spray Adhesive (see Resources, page 111) on a piece of batting and backing fabric I had layered together. I arranged the blocks on this base and they held fast long enough to do some straight-line stitching across the piece. After everything was held in place, it was faster and easier to continue quilting. Edges of the blocks stick up here and there, and some of the fabric frays, but I am happy with that look. Some of my clothing and accessories have fraying on them, and now I have a quilt that does the same thing.

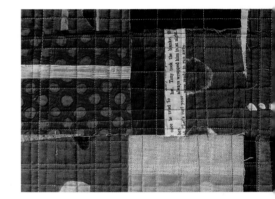

I used thread of varying weights, from 50-weight to 28-weight, because I wanted the stitching to stand out, and the 28-weight thread does that. I was also able to use a very heavy-weight Kreinik Silk Bella thread (see Resources, page 111) on my machine, which adds a bit of shine.

Detail of stitching

There were a few places where slivers of batting showed, so I fused some slivers of fabric to cover it up. After I looked at these little added bits, I decided to add a few more—I liked the way they helped to draw the eye from one block to the next. These act in the same way as "coping strips" do in pieced blocks.

Fused slivers

Why It Works

All the blocks in *Cut Up* have a similar, though not identical, shape. I try for close, not exact. Little coping strips are put where they are needed and as a bonus add some additional color. These thin little lines draw the eye from one block to the next.

The quilt uses very few pure colors. If you look at the Ultimate 3-in-1 Color Tool, most of the colors I used appear at the bottom of the pure color—they are very dark shades of yellow, chartreuse, aqua blue, and red-violet. Some colors are pushed to almost the neighboring color, but most remain on the dark side. My original focus fabric does contain some glimpses of yellow, but it is not a pure yellow. Besides, a lot depends on what color the color is next to.

The two-ply gauze has a somewhat dull appearance, as does the rustic cloth from Africa. Hemp burlap has a shiny surface and is not at all like the dark blue regular burlap I used. Silk and the silk/linen blend are shinier than the hemp burlap and reflect light. All of these different appearances and textures provide variety and add movement to the quilt.

Repetition also plays a big part in this quilt. There are large dots and small ones. Some are obvious and some you really have to look for. The dull gold dots that are painted on a piece of mauve African fabric are quite subtle, while the irregular dots on the dark green fabric show quite well.

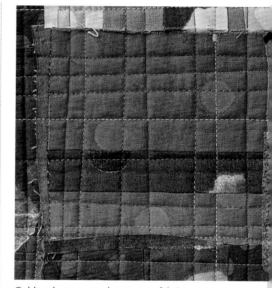

Golden dots stamped on mauve fabric

Would I make another quilt this way again? Probably. I enjoyed painting on the fabric and have most of the bugs worked out. I also like the idea of the blocks not being completely attached to the batting/backing layer and the technique of letting fabric ravel. It adds texture. And last, including fabrics you normally wouldn't use is something you should try.

WENDY'S QUILT:
Confluence

SURFACE STITCHING, THREAD TEXTURING, AND CREATING NEW FABRIC ...

Confluence by Wendy Hill, 30" × 19"

In the Beginning

More than twenty years ago, a chance suggestion by my husband to "do that thread thing" with a stalled project led me to develop my own methods of thread texturing and surface stitching. Today I'm known for having a lot more thread than fabric in my walk-in closet.

For this challenge, I really wanted to go back to my roots with thread while at the same time exploiting what I know now after all these years about actual stitching styles and techniques, products such as water-soluble stabilizers, and methods to

avoid or fix warping. I planned to make "new" fabric with collage and thread texturing, but I felt open to all sorts of possibilities in creating the surface texture and design.

Original sketch

Ideas seem to come to me while my linear brain is preoccupied. I sketch and make notes as soon as possible so I won't lose my mental grip on the idea. Later I can develop the idea and refine the sketch.

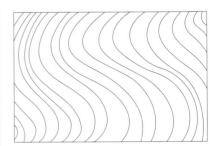

Refined sketch, enlarged to 28"× 19" (a 3:2 aspect ratio)

Focus fabric

Color and Design Decisions

A photograph of a marsh with cattails in the late fall sent me in the direction of a color scheme. I imagined lots of yellows and yellow-greens with burnt orange-reds and possibly some blues. This, along with a piece of fabric by Melody Miller (from her Mustang collection for Cotton + Steel), led me to find my own combination of fabrics and thread. I looked to the color families in the horse fabric, but I chose my own variations of these colors for my quilt.

Coordinating fabrics

 TIP

Using a Focus Fabric

Using the horse print as a focus fabric to pull together coordinating fabrics is not a new trick. Sometimes the focus fabric is used in the quilt, sometimes it isn't. I chose not to use the focus fabric in the quilt. It's amazing how many different looks can be created when starting with the same focus fabric. This could be an idea for a new challenge among your quilting friends.

Coordinating threads

I made six pieces of "new" fabric with raw-edge collaging and thread texturing using Sulky Paper Solvy as the base. This product (and others like it, such as Sulky Fabri-Solvy or Sulky Solvy; see Resources, page 111) provides a temporary base for thread texturing in order to get good stitch quality.

Photos by Wendy Hill

Under Construction

I planned to make a lot of pieced units, sew the units together into a quilt top, quilt to batting, cut up the quilt top, thread texture the wavy sections, and then put it all back together again. If anyone thinks buying yardage to cut up and sew back together is crazy, then my plan is even crazier.

Trial and Evaluation

Without thinking too much, I started making a lot of units. One of the units caught my attention; I made as many as I could with my limited scraps of the watery fabric, using ladder-type piecing. I didn't need to know how they would come together to keep making more units.

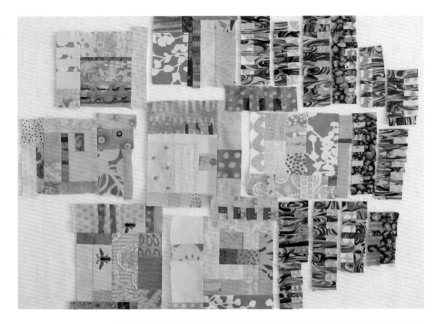

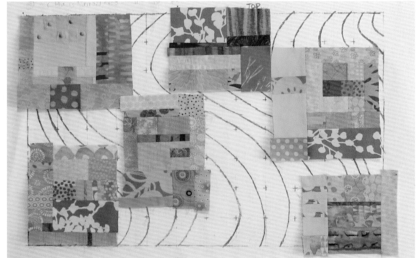

Piece or Collage?

At this point, I had to decide whether to raw-edge collage the units together or piece them (right sides together). I decided to piece them together and add more thread texturing later. Next came basting the pieced top to the batting with water-soluble thread, surface stitching (page 101), and quilting to the batting only (page 97) with neon yellow thread.

Blocks pieced together

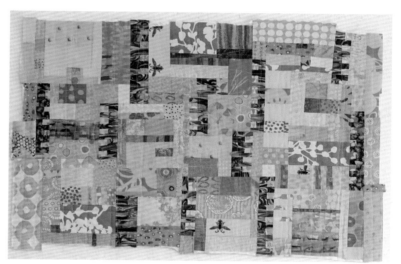

Surface stitching

Quilted to batting only

Photos by Wendy Hill

Making the Leap

I loved the quilt so much at this point that I had a few moments of self-doubt about cutting it up. But I had to persevere to bring my idea to life, so I took a deep breath and forged ahead. After modifying my full-size drawing to make the wavy sections larger in a few places, I traced the pattern onto freezer paper to make templates. I machine basted the cut wavy sections to Sulky Fabri-Solvy with water-soluble thread. After thread texturing the sections, I finished the edges with my satin-stitched edge finish (page 99).

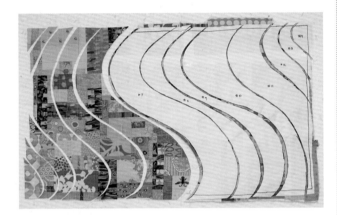

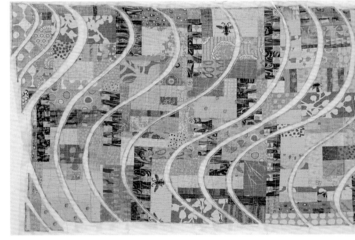

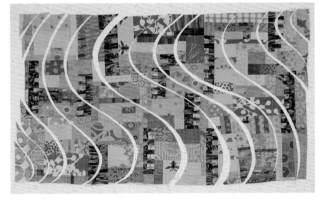

Photos by Wendy Hill

Joining or Covering the Curves

After washing out all the water-soluble products and drying the curved sections, I discovered that my plan to join the sections with half-zippers (as piping) could not work.

Even if the wavy sections fit together perfectly (they didn't), the half-zippers would not bend around the tighter curves.

I got around this roadblock by deciding to cover the curves with self-made bias tape to connect the sections. First, I fused the sections together, from the back, with cut strips of fusible interfacing. Then I stitched the bias strips in place from the front. I discovered a unique finish to the outside edge by folding the bias strips back on themselves, creating a contemporary-style Prairie Points edge finish at the ends.

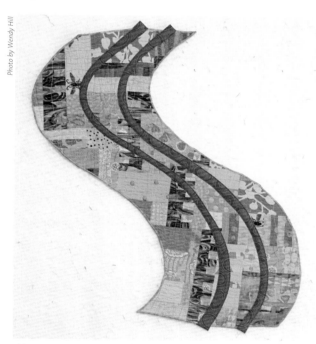

Photo by Wendy Hill

I liked the look of the bias tape, even though it covers up the finished edges.

TIP

Working with Bias Tape

I have found that hand basting the edges of bias tape with big stitches allows you to stitch smoothly and continuously, without fiddling with removing the pins.

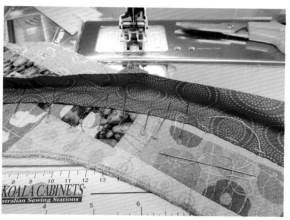

The bias tape wants to bend around the curves.

Photos by Wendy Hill

Hand basting with basting thread (see Resources, page 111) allows you to stitch continuously and smoothly.

When I finished with the quilt top, I realized the red-orange was too much of a good thing. I tried covering it up completely, but then I missed the effect this color had on the entire composition. Finally, I tried a narrower bias strip on top, leaving a narrow strip of red-orange on both sides, which was just the right amount.

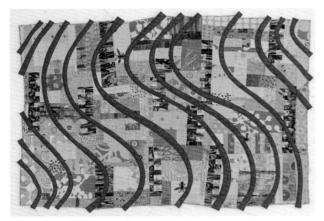

Original red bias strips

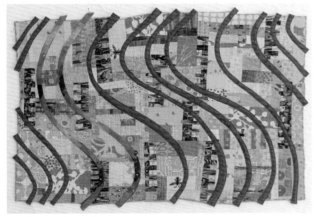

Bias strips completely covered up

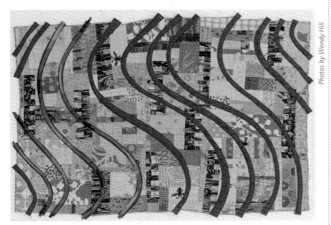

Narrower bias strips on top of original bias strips

I repeated the process of bending, pinning, basting, and stitching the new bias tape in place. I let the red-orange bias tape show along the edge, like piping, but in irregular widths on purpose. The quilt top was now completely finished.

This is the best solution among all the ideas and plans.

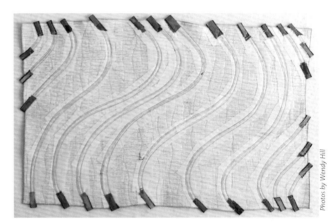

The finished quilt top from the back: batting, fusible interfacing, stitching lines

Because I wanted to keep the irregular edges, wool felt was the perfect material for the back. I added more quilting through all the layers, following the edges of the bias tape and the outside edges. Because felt does not ravel, I was able to trim the outside edge next to the stitching lines. After many twists and turns, the quilt is finally finished!

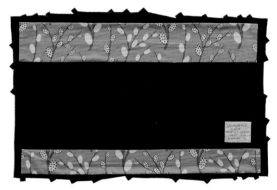

Wool felt on the back allowed me to cut along the irregular edges without fear of raveling.

LOVE/HATE

At the beginning of the design process, there are infinite possibilities in front of us. It's an exciting time in the process of making a quilt. But as forks in the road appear, and left or right turns get taken, the path to the finish line starts to narrow. As the quilt takes shape, the grandiose idea of what it *might have been* is slowly being replaced by *what the quilt actually is*. This is a time when an original love for the idea can sour. Our brain needs to catch up, adapt, and adjust to the reality of the quilt compared with the image in our heads. It's important to persevere at this stage so the project doesn't stall and look so bleak it's never picked up again. Yes, it's exhilarating putting together a fabric collection and beginning the project, but after a quilt is finished, that excitement generally returns.

Why It Works

Finishing the quilt project not only feels good but also gives you time to reconnect with the quilt and reflect on the experience. The more you understand the principles of color and design as well as your own personal design process, the better you can direct your skills and knowledge toward turning your ideas into finished quilts. Intuition is not a mysterious quality; it's the result of learning from your experiences and drawing from your knowledge base. Good judgment comes from experience, but experience is the *sum total* of what goes both *right* and *wrong*.

This quilt has all the movement and flow that my quilts seem to embody. Every component contributes in some way to the overall effect. It's a good lesson in remembering that everything in the composition should have a purpose. I had grand ideas about using zippers, making fabric coils, painting fabric, and more, but editing is always key to a successful quilt.

- The assorted mix of fabrics in the background piecing works together well. The colors read as a dominant acid yellow and green, yet the wide assortment of other colors, styles, and values works in the mix. The overlay of striped bias tape seals the deal.

- There is variety in the range of scale of the motifs and the cut sizes of the fabrics in the background.

- The narrow, vertical strip-pieced "ladder" units unify the entire composition. Imagine the background without those units: the whole thing dies of boredom.

- Reassembling the curved sections offsets the lines and shapes just enough to make your eyes work harder (in a good way) to make sense of the patterns.

- The narrow edge of red-orange along the bias tape is just enough to add a tingle of excitement while connecting all the reds in the background.

- The striped bias tape (on top of the red-orange) pulls the composition together while pushing it apart at the same time. The movement of the colors in the stripe adds a design layer all by itself. But the movement of color found in the bias tape also unifies the entire composition.

Special Techniques

BINDING

Reversible Double-Fold Binding

Quilts: *ColorBlind* (page 18), *Color Blinded Again* (page 60)

This binding, with two different fabrics, is treated like any other double French-fold binding. The cut widths of the binding vary with the thickness of the fabrics and batting as well as your preferred seam allowance / binding width. Just do what I always do: Start with the following measurements and adjust as needed. I primarily use Quilters Dream Cotton Request Loft batting and a ⅜″ seam allowance / binding width.

> **TIP**
>
> **Check Your Measurements**
>
> To check your measurements, make a sample length of binding a few inches long. Sew this piece of binding to your quilt (use big stitches for easy removal); the binding should fold over between the two fabrics and just cover the stitching line on the back of the quilt. Adjust the measurements as needed.

1. Cut strips of fabric using the following measurements by the length needed to make enough binding for your quilt. (Sew together multiple strips first as needed to get the desired length.)

Fabric 1: 2⅛″ wide

Fabric 2: 1⅛″ wide

2. Using a ¼″ seam allowance, sew the two fabrics right sides together. *You must use this seam allowance and press the seam open* for this method to work.

3. Fold the binding in half lengthwise and press a crease along the fold. Place the narrow side of the binding to the "right side" of the quilt and sew, using your planned seam allowance. Finish the binding using your favorite method.

Machine Topstitched Binding

Quilts: *ColorBlind* (page 18), *Color Blinded Again* (page 60)

Adapt your favorite method of making double French-fold binding so that the binding overlaps the stitching line by almost ⅛″ (on the back of the quilt). If it seems like this method takes more time than blindstitching by hand, then perhaps you are fast with your hand sewing! New methods always take a little practice.

1. Sew the binding to the quilt as usual, mitering the corners.

2. Fold the binding to the back, making sure the fold overlaps the stitching line, and pin or clip.

3. After the binding is pinned or clipped in place, blindstitch the four mitered corners in place, stitching about 1″ in each direction from the corners. From experience, I've learned that mitered corners tend to shift with basting only.

Blind stitches

4. Use a basting thread (see Basting, page 64, and Resources, page 111) to hand sew a long running stitch (about ¼″ to ½″) along the very edge of the fold of the binding on the back of the quilt.

Basting stitches

Stitch consistently along the edge—this is the line you will follow from the front.

5. Turn the quilt over to the front. The basting line shows you exactly where the fold of the binding is on the back of the quilt. By stitching between the basting line and the ditch of the binding seam, you'll always be stitching along the fold of the binding on the back of the quilt.

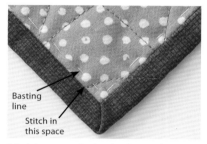

Basting line

Stitch in this space

Stitch between the basting line and the binding from the front of the quilt.

6. Machine topstitch through all the layers (from the front of the quilt), using a walking foot and a matching or blending thread color. Continue to stitch a consistent line between the basting thread and the binding around all sides of the quilt, pivoting at the corners.

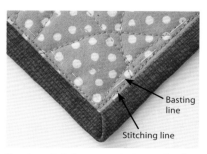

Basting line

Stitching line

Consistently follow your chosen sewing line.

7. When you are finished with the stitching, run the thread tails through the binding. Remove the basting thread. Check the *back* for accuracy—the machine topstitching should run parallel to the fold of the binding, without slipping off the edge. The topstitching is barely visible from the front. *Note:* I often stitch closer to the ditch to hide the stitching even more.

Topstitching from the back of the quilt

The topstitching is barely visible from the front of the quilt.

TIP

Imperfections

- You might find gaps on the back of the quilt, where the topstitching doesn't catch the binding. Ignore small gaps of a stitch or two. Longer gaps should get sewn again (or blind stitched in place). Practice makes perfect with this technique.

- This is a good technique for quilts given away as a donation to a cause or as gifts in which the quilt will take many trips through the washer and dryer.

FACING FINISH

Quilts: *Stepping Out* (page 6), *Bright Hopes 2* (page 7), *Snow Strings* (page 28), *Silent Reflection* (page 40), *Echino Yet Again* (page 50), *One Orange Dot* (page 61), *Cut Up* (page 72)

Between the two of us, we have finished quilts with piping, satin stitching, binding, and of course, facings. A facing gives the edge a clean finish, but lumpy corners detract from the final look—this method avoids the lumpy corners.

Plan ahead for a ½˝ seam allowance. The wider seam allowance makes the edges fold flatter compared with a narrow seam allowance, which tries to pop up. The focus with this method is on getting the bulk out of the corners.

Cutting the Pieces

1. Cut 4 strips total, each 2⅝˝ wide by the total measurement of each quilt side, minus 10˝. Fold the strips in half lengthwise and press.

2. Using the facing corner pattern (page 104), cut a total of 4 corners from the same fabric as the strips. Fold the short ends over, wrong sides together, about ¼˝ to ⅜˝. Press.

Sewing Facing Pieces to the Quilt Top

1. Pin the 4 corner units to the quilt top, right sides together. Position the folded strips on the sides of the quilt, overlapping the ends by ⅜˝ to ½˝ with the folded edges of the corner units. Sew the facing pieces to the quilt top using a ½˝ seam allowance.

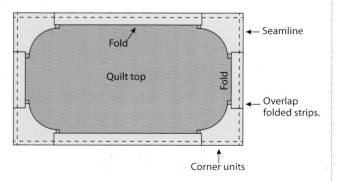

Fold

Quilt top

Fold

Seamline

Overlap folded strips.

Corner units

2. Press the facing away from the quilt top, pushing the facing strip over the seam allowance. The corner facing unit makes it snug, but push the nose of the iron as far as you can into the corner to continue pressing the facing away from the quilt top.

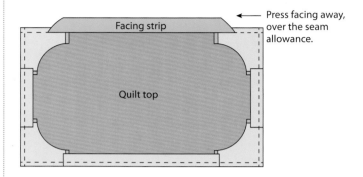

Facing strip

Quilt top

Press facing away, over the seam allowance.

3. *Understitch*—which is actually topstitching on the facing and through all of the layers (facing and seam allowance)—next to the seamline. This kind of stitching next to the seamline (the ditch) helps make the facing stay on the inside and form a clean knife edge. Start and end as far into the corner as possible, stitching very close to the seamline.

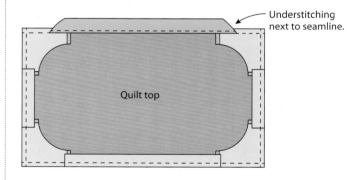

Quilt top

Understitching next to seamline.

Reducing the Bulk in the Corners

1. Rip out the stitching lines about 1˝–1½˝ from the corner in both directions.

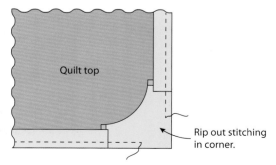

Quilt top

Rip out stitching in corner.

2. Peel back the quilt top and the facing *only*, leaving the batting exposed (and fabric backing intact). You'll probably see the needle holes in the batting showing the stitching line.

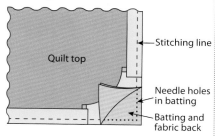

3. Trim across the corner, at about a 45° angle, about ⅛″ on the *inside* of the corner. This removes the bulk of the batting and fabric from the corner, making it easier to turn the facing right side out. So you're actually cutting the tip of the backing and batting out of the corner, along with the seam allowance around the corner.

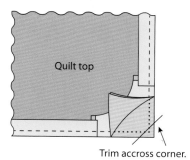

Check twice, cut once—through batting and fabric backing only.

Finishing the Facing

1. Replace the quilt top and facing fabrics. Sew the corners again, over the same stitching line as before. Try turning the corner. If it is still bulky, trim the seam allowances on either side of the corner. Cover the corner with your thumbnail to avoid accidentally cutting too much. Repeat to finish all four corners the same way.

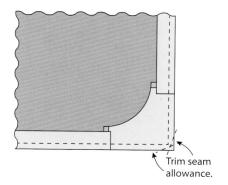

2. Turn the facing to the back, carefully turning and pushing out the corners. Use a blunt tool (rounded end, not sharp) to push out the corner bit by bit, or pull on the corner with a pin to tug the corner into place, or both! The corner should be at right angles, not pointy like a party hat. If the corner isn't right or to your liking, turn the facing back again, smooth out, and start over with turning the facing right side out. Smooth the fabric out and trim more bulk if needed. The corner can improve the second time around. The sides should fold over cleanly, with no facing showing on the quilt top and no quilt top showing on the back.

3. Pin the facing in place on all four sides, turning under the edges of the corner unit so the edge of the corner lines up with the folded edge of the strip. Blindstitch (page 17) the facing in place.

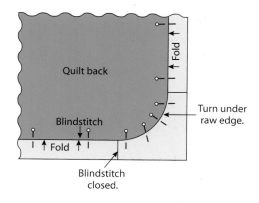

Faced corner from the back of *Snow Strings* (page 28)

Faced corner from the front of *Snow Strings* (page 28)

FREE-FORM SAWTOOTH STARS

Quilt: *Color Blinded Again* (page 60)

Sawtooth Stars are drafted on an unequal nine-patch grid. The eight outer units (four corner squares and four star point rectangles) are always half the height of (and the same width as) the center square. This basic relationship is retained with free-form Sawtooth Stars, but the points do not meet exactly at the outer edges, the points vary in height and angle, and the size of the finished square varies with each star.

 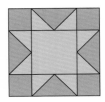 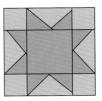

Grid for   Traditional   Free-form
Sawtooth Star   Sawtooth Star   Sawtooth Star

The following instructions will yield a free-form star approximately 5½˝ square. If you want the stars to finish larger or smaller, cut the units larger or smaller.

Cutting for Star Points

Cut the star-point fabric units about 1˝ larger than the background fabric units for more freedom in skewing the points.

- -

1. Cut 8 background squares about the same size (3˝). Cut a center square from the star fabric the same size as the background fabric (3˝). Cut 4 larger squares from the star fabric (4˝), and then cut on the diagonal to make 8 triangles. Set aside 4 of the background squares.

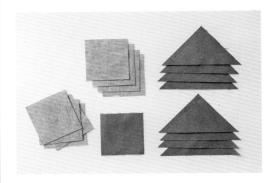

2. Start making the 4 star-point units using all 8 star fabric triangles and the 4 remaining background squares. Position a triangle right sides together with the background, so that when flipped over, the star fabric covers the background fabric, forming a star point.

3. Trim the excess background fabric. Press the seam open.

4. Position the second triangle as described (previous page). Trim the excess background fabric. Press the seam open. Repeat these steps to make a total of 4 geese or star-point units. *Note:* Position the triangles slightly differently each time to get randomly shaped star points.

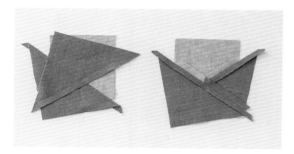

5. Square-up all 4 star-point units. Position the grid ruler across the bottom so that you leave a seam allowance below the V; trim off excess. Position the grid ruler to trim off excess fabric beyond the background fabric on both sides, and trim. *Don't do anything to the top edge.*

6. Arrange the block. Line up the units so the inner horizontal seamlines are even. Sew the units together. Press seams open.

7. Look for the tallest star point and add your seam allowance (plus a bit extra—⅛″–¼″ more) to the measurement. Use this measurement to square-up the block.

INSET SQUARES

Quilt: *Stepping Out* (page 6)

Inset squares take some practice, but the effect of the inner square floating in the outer square makes it worth it—get started with these basic directions. Choose tightly woven fabrics for your first attempts (less chance of raveling). Adapt the measurements and fabric styles for your next project with inset squares or rectangles.

1. Choose two fabrics with good color and value contrast. Cut a 4˝ square from each fabric. Cut a 2˝ square template from freezer paper.

2. Stack the fabric squares, both right sides up, with the fabric for the outer square on top and the fabric for the inset square on the bottom. Position the freezer-paper template on the top square and press. Machine baste around the template, using the longest stitch setting possible and making sure to pivot on the corners.

3. Remove the template. From inside the stitching on the top piece of fabric, pinch the top fabric away from the bottom fabric and cut a slit in the middle. Insert the scissors between the layers to cut a big X, stopping precisely at each corner. Do not cut into the basting.

Cutting accurate, straight lines makes the process easier, especially if this is your first inset square.

4. Sew one side at a time. Remove the basting along one stitching line (from corner to corner). Tuck the triangle flap of the fabric underneath, while flipping the outer square right sides together, making the triangle flap flat on the background fabric. Sew from corner to corner. Open up and finger-press.

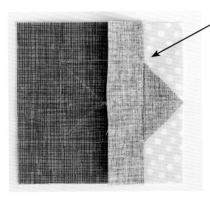

Stitching line

Do not stitch over the fold at the top and bottom, but don't leave a gap between the fold and the cut corner.

Doing this step is easier than reading about it.

5. Repeat with the other three sides, starting with the opposite side first. Finger-press as you sew. A final pressing at the end makes the block look sharp; avoid heavy-handed ironing, which will stretch the fabric. Trim the triangle flaps and background square, leaving a generous seam allowance (about ⅜″).

Always sew opposite sides first.

Finished inset squares

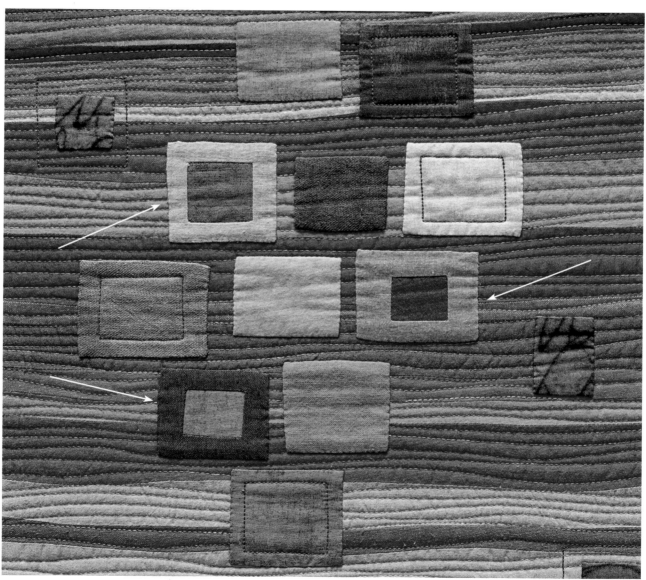

Sample inset squares from the quilt *Stepping Out*

PRESSING ADVICE AND SEAM TREATMENTS

Step-by-step ironing may be an overlooked tip, but good pressing skills are key to the look of your finished quilts. Don't be afraid to use steam or spritzed water on the fabric or ironing board. Just remember to place and press with the iron without sliding and gliding. If you've never tried pressing seams open or pressing with a clapper, please try it. We believe you'll like the results.

Pressing Seams Open

We strongly advocate pressing seams open to reduce bulk. When quilters sewed seams by hand, the seams had to be pressed over for added strength. But machine-stitched seams don't need this special treatment.

Using a Wider Seam Allowance

We both use wider seam allowances than the typical ¼". When Pat is string piecing, she uses a generous ½" (not strictly measured) seam allowance. The extra seam allowance is handy if she needs to alter the way things are fitting together.

When Wendy is piecing cut shapes that require a standard seam allowance, she uses a 5⁄16" seam allowance, which doubles to a convenient 5⁄8". This odd figure is the actual distance between the needle and the edge of the primary sewing foot on her BERNINA 155. When drafting patterns, Wendy sews around the shape—with just the needle and no thread—to mark the cutting lines on the template. When she is not following a block pattern, she also sews with a generous 3⁄8"–½" seam allowance for the same reasons as Pat.

Using a Clapper

We both press with steam and a hardwood clapper. As a self-taught quilter from ages ago, Wendy applied her tailoring skills to making quilts, including pressing with a clapper. Pat adopted the method when she saw the difference for herself.

Apply the heat and steam to the pressed-open seam allowance with one hand. Lift off the iron and, with the other hand, cover the pressed spot with the clapper. Hold the clapper in place for a few seconds. This holds in the heat and moisture without scorching the fabric. Adapt these instructions for right- or left-handed pressing.

Press first, with or without steam. Wendy and Pat usually use steam.

Purchase or make your own hardwood clapper.

Lift up the iron and immediately cover the area with the clapper. Hold for a few seconds.

Two Seam Treatments

Stitch the Seams in Place

When your step-by-step pressing starts to mess up all the previous pressing, try stitching the major seams in place with water-soluble thread (such as Vanish-Lite by Superior, page 111). In addition to stabilizing the growing quilt top, the stitched seams usually prevent having to press the entire quilt top before layering the quilt sandwich. The water-soluble thread washes out.

Fuse the Seams in Place

Sometimes seams just don't want to stay open, especially when made from heavy fabrics or at intersections where a lot of seams come together. When you can't use water-soluble thread to stitch the seams open (because the quilt will not get washed later), fuse cut strips of fusible interfacing over the seams to hold them in place. For example, with *Cairn Study 3*, the stiff hair interfacing didn't want to stay pressed no matter how much steam or clapping I applied. Cut your own strips from fusible interfacing yardage or buy precut strips on a roll, such as Make It Simpler Fusible Interfacing (by C&T Publishing; see Resources, page 111).

QUILTING-AS-YOU-SEW: TWO WAYS

Quilting-as-You-Sew with Seam Covers

Quilts: *ColorBlind* (page 18), *Cairn Study 3* (page 29), *Color Blinded Again* (page 60)

There are a variety of reasons to construct a quilt in sections and then sew the sections together. Since you have to add a fabric backing anyway, consider making the quilt reversible.

The first method—making and quilting in blocks or sections, sewing together the blocks/sections *right sides together*, and *covering* the seams on the other side with self-made seam covers, gives you options with the composition. The seam covers can blend in or become part of the design, masquerading as sashing (as with *Color Blinded Again*). We love solutions to problems that become an advantage.

The Steps

1. Place and pin the two quilted sections *right sides together*. Stitch the seam.

Photo by Wendy Hill

2. Press the seams open. If the layers are thick, zigzag the edge of the seam *at this point* to squish the batting. (If you zigzag before sewing the seam, it will probably stretch the edge of the quilt.) Whipstitch the seams down, stitching through the batting only. This keeps the seam from popping open under the seam cover.

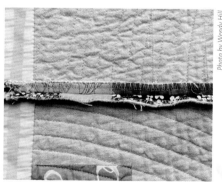

Photo by Wendy Hill

Serged edge and whipstitching

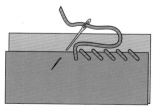

Since your whipstitching will be hidden by the seam covers, you can work quickly, making stitches farther apart.

3. Make the seam covers from cut strips of the chosen fabric. Determine the width of the strips this way:

- Measure the width of the pressed-open seam allowance.

- Add ½″.

- Multiply this number by 2.

Cut strips and sew them together as needed to make them long enough. Lightly press the strip in half lengthwise, then fold the long edges to the middle and press a sharp crease.

For this example, cut the strip 2¼″ wide: ⅝″ (width of the pressed-open seam allowance) + ½″ = 1⅛″, multiplied by 2).

4. Pin the seam covering in place, keeping the ends out of the next intersection to reduce bulk. Blindstitch (page 17) the seam cover in place.

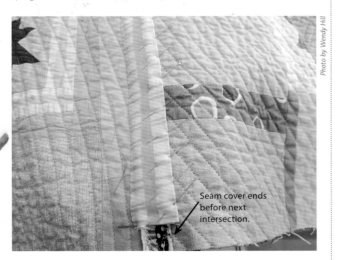

Seam cover ends before next intersection.

5. At the next intersection, trim the bulk out of the seam allowance by clipping it.

Clip bulk out of seam allowance.

6. Continue covering the seams until the quilt is fully assembled. If the quilt is reversible, consider making a reversible binding as well (page 86).

TIP

Seam Cover Considerations

- For reversible quilts, you decide which side gets sewn *right sides together* and which side has the seam covers.

- Make the seam covers disappear by using fabric that matches or blends in with the quilt. *Or* use contrasting fabrics for the seam covers to look like sashing or part of the composition.

TIP

Cons and Pros

If you never ever do any hand stitching, then this method has limited appeal. However, there are a few circumstances, with advance planning, in which the seam coverings can be machine topstitched. The stitching line—seen on the other side—accents the composition in the way you've planned.

Even if you enjoy or don't mind hand sewing, it might seem as if this shortcut is actually the long way around. Think of it as a way to quilt a large quilt on your home sewing machine or as a way to make a quilt reversible. It's another option to add to your bag of tricks and techniques.

Quilting-as-You-Sew to Batting

Quilts: *Silent Reflection* (page 40), *Ripple Effect* (page 51), *Confluence* (page 73)

Wendy started quilting to batting when she first learned how to free-motion quilt so she could cover up the terrible stitch quality on the back with the real fabric backing. But Wendy and Pat love the other reasons to quilt to batting first:

- It's easier to handle smaller sections.

- When quilting or thread texturing, especially with uneven densities of stitching, working in sections with batting only helps prevent warping of the entire quilt top.

- It's easy to deal with thread tails (the stops and starts of a stitching or quilting line). Just pull the thread to the back and tie off. The ugly knots get covered up with the fabric backing. This gives you more freedom with your stitching.

TIP
- -

Working on Batting

- Check your bobbin case for lint more often when stitching to batting.

- Use a walking foot or your basic foot, whichever gives the best stitch quality.

- Plan for a wider seam allowance (up to ⅜″) and press seams open with a clapper (page 94). If the seams want to pop closed again, whipstitch them in place through the batting only (page 95) or hold in place with cut strips of fusible interfacing.

- Explore thread texturing (page 100) as a way to create surface texture with various kinds of stitching and stitches found on your sewing machine.

- -

The Steps

1. Baste the quilt top to the batting, using your favorite method. Most of the time we use spray basting, with or without a grid stitched with water-soluble thread (see Basting, page 64).

2. Quilt or thread texture through the layers (quilt top and batting). When quilting to the batting in sections (or with small quilts), it's easy to block the section (or quilt top) with steam before the final assembly. This way, the final quilt is flat and not warped. Here are two samples, back and front:

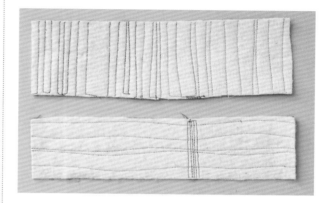

3. Take advantage of this method to tie off the thread tails on the back. These get covered up later with the fabric backing. When Pat quilts random grid lines, she often stops somewhere in the quilt top. Maybe she wants to change the thread color or density (for example, one stitching line stops and two stitching lines carry on). Quilting to batting lets you be more impulsive with your stitching lines because the tails get tied off on the back.

Wendy likes to stitch echo quilting lines (see Echo Quilting with a Walking Foot, page 70), often in arcs. Quilting to batting lets her quilt closely spaced, roughly parallel lines with the ease of tying off the tails on the back or backstitching on the outside edge of the section. The stitch length stays consistent (no stitching tiny stitches at the end of the line), nor are there tedious thread tails to knot and lead through the batting.

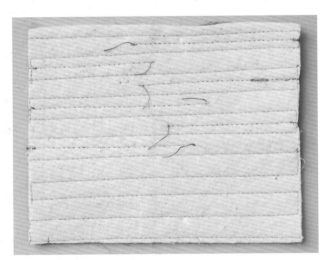

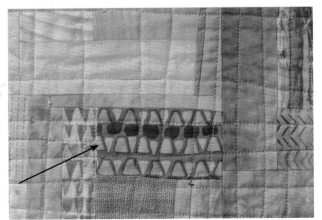

Bright Hopes 2 (page 7). Look for the stitching lines that come to a stop. These small changes add up to large overall effects.

4. If you break up a quilt into sections, just sew the sections *right sides together* using a wider seam allowance. Press the seams open. If the seams want to pop up, whipstitch them in place through the batting only. Continue to sew the sections together until you've assembled the entire quilt top. Here is an example, back and front:

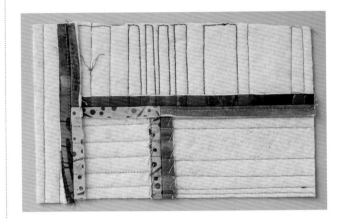

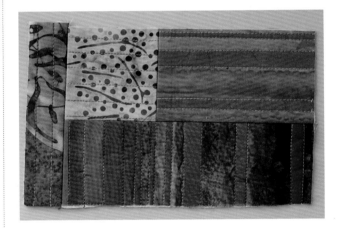

5. Baste the fabric backing to the quilted top/batting. Add enough additional quilting to hold the layers together securely. For wall quilts, not much additional quilting is required. For functional quilts, add enough quilting through all the layers so the quilt will hold up to use, abuse, and a trip or two through the washer and dryer.

PROFESSIONAL-LOOKING SATIN-STITCHED EDGE FINISH

Quilts: *Cairn Study 3* (page 29), *Square Dance* (page 41), *Confluence* (page 73)

Wendy developed her satin-stitch edge finish a decade ago when she began making fiber art postcards. Later she began using this method to finish the edges of some of her quilts. Avoid the pitfalls that Wendy made while learning how to do a good satin stitch! *Note:* Apply the same principles when satin stitching around shapes.

The trick for a flawless, rounded satin stitch is to go around the edge a total of three times. Set your machine to zigzag. Begin the first round with a narrow width setting and longer length setting. With each round, the width setting gets wider and the length setting gets shorter. The result is a plump, rounded satin stitch with no clumping and no gaps.

Wendy uses Sulky Blendables 30-weight variegated thread (see Resources, page 111) with her BERNINA 155 to finish the edges of quilts and postcards. You'll need to adjust the settings for your sewing machine, your thread choice (weight and fiber content), and the thickness of the quilt or postcard. Leave the thread tails hanging to mark the start of the next round. When finished, run the thread tails through the satin stitching and then clip.

Here are three examples of satin-stitched finished edges:

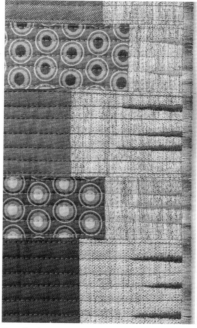

Detail of *Cairn Study 3* (page 29)

Detail of *Square Dance* (page 41)

Detail of *Confluence* (page 73)

Round 1: *Width:* 2. *Length:* 2.

Round 2: *Width:* Add three clicks. *Length:* Subtract four clicks.

Round 3: *Width:* Add three clicks. *Length:* Subtract three or four clicks.

THREAD TEXTURING, SURFACE STITCHING, AND SATIN-STITCHED TRIANGLES

Thread Texturing

Quilts: *Bright Hopes 2* (page 7), *Square Dance* (page 41), *Confluence* (page 73)

Thread texturing does just what it says—adds texture to your quilt while allowing you to add color and, if you like, stitching (quilting) through all the layers, all at the same time. Experiment with the decorative and utility stitches that come with your machine. Alter the default settings or use the stitch as is. Alternate the decorative stitch with straight stitching either by programming the stitches into the machine's memory or by manually switching back and forth.

Here are a few of our favorite thread texturing stitches:

- Alternate a straight stitch with random or planned bursts of satin stitching.

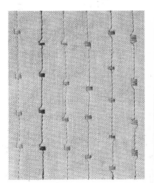  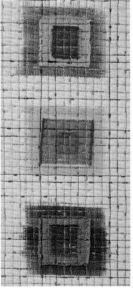

From left to right: Sulky Poly Deco, Aurifil cotton 40-weight, Madeira rayon, Madeira Polyneon, Sulky Blendables 30-weight (two lines on far right)

Detail of *Bright Hopes 2* (page 7)

Detail of *Square Dance* (page 41)

- Look for a wavy line or serpentine stitch on your sewing machine. On some BERNINA machines, this is Stitch #4, a stitched zigzag (running stitch) used for darning, that, when altered, stitches an undulating line. It's a great stitch for quilting, but keep it in mind for adding thread texture too. Try alternating bursts of satin stitching for even more texture.

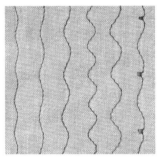

Sulky Blendables 30-weight

- When stitching a straight stitch, manually hit reverse off and on, in quick succession, several times. The machine will stitch forward—backward—forward—backward (and so on), creating a raised bump or slub in the stitching line. The more you repeat the process, the thicker the slub. Wendy calls this stitch "ee-ee" (imagine saying "ee-ee" while hitting reverse and letting go).

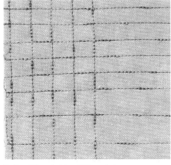

Sulky Blendables 30-weight

Detail of *Confluence* (page 73), showing wavy-line stitch with bursts of satin stitching

Surface Stitching

Quilt: *Confluence* (page 73)

Wendy developed this method of stitching hand-steered wavy lines to uniformly distribute stitched lines over the surface of a quilt. When you need to finish the quilting in a hurry, this method is easy (and therefore fast) and looks great. Use surface stitching to add thread texture to make new fabric or to stitch through all the layers. The result is a pleasing uniform density of stitching.

Use the straight stitch setting with the feed dogs engaged and the needle in the center position, with a walking or basic foot. Hold the fabric or basted quilt with your hands at approximately 10 and 12 o'clock and hand-steer to stitch wavy lines. Imagine you are skiing down a slope or weaving through orange cones while driving on a road. Make tight or gradual curves and stitch them parallel or in a grid, or let them overlap. For this method, keep the styles of the curves and the distance between curves consistent once you start. Use one thread or a variety of threads. These samples are stitched with Sulky Blendables 30-weight variegated thread.

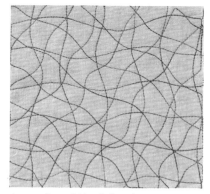

A wavy-line grid in all directions

Overlapped surface stitching lines to make new fabric for *Confluence*

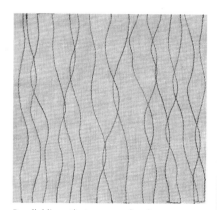

Parallel lines that cross each other randomly

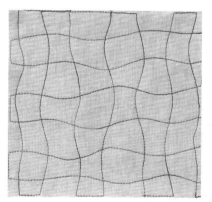

A wavy-line grid with vertical and horizontal lines

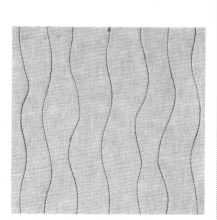

Roughly parallel vertical wavy lines

A wavy-line grid on the diagonal

Look for the bright yellow surface-stitched lines evenly distributed across the quilt composition.

Satin-Stitched Triangles

Quilts: *Cairn Study 3* (page 29), *Cairn Study* (page 34)

Before you try this on a quilt, practice with your sewing machine first to find the right combination of zigzag setting with your thread and fabric or quilt base. To make these shapes, you'll need one hand on the button or dial to decrease the stitch width and one hand to steer the fabric.

TIP

Working with Satin Stitch

■ Because of the variables, you'll always need to experiment on samples before stitching the triangles on the real thing.

■ The combination of the initial width of the satin stitch, the motor speed, and the decreasing stitch width determines the shape of the triangle.

■ Thicker thread forms a satin stitch with a longer stitch length compared with a thinner thread. Compare stitch length settings on a practice fabric base before stitching the real thing.

■ It would be difficult to make identical triangles, but I'm sure there are some who could do it with enough practice. I'm not one of them, so I've found enjoyment in the variety of shapes.

---

1. Start with the widest stitch width at the top of the triangle.

2. Let the needle swing back and forth a few times before starting to decrease the stitch width.

3. If your sewing machine has a dial, turn it slowly and evenly. For machines with buttons, push the button repetitively as if timed to the tick-tock of a metronome.

4. As the triangle comes to a point, speed up the rate of decreasing the stitch width. Stop when the triangle comes to a point (stitch width 0).

5. Tie off thread tails on the back of the fabric or run the tails through the batting of the quilt.

6. Experiment with different shapes and thread types.

7. Registration lines are helpful when making triangles along the edge of the fabric or quilt, as Wendy did. Mark two parallel lines along the edge. Start stitching the triangle at the first line. When the needle crosses the second line, start decreasing the width to form the triangle.

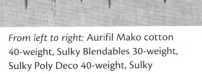

From left to right: Aurifil Mako cotton 40-weight, Sulky Blendables 30-weight, Sulky Poly Deco 40-weight, Sulky Blendables, Sulky Blendables, Sulky Poly Deco 40-weight, Aurifil Mako cotton 40-weight, Mettler 60-weight / 2 ply, Mettler 50-weight / 3 ply, Mettler Poly Sheen

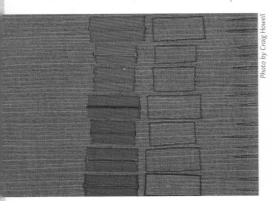

Detail of *Cairn Study*

Photo by Craig Howell

Detail of *Cairn Study 3*

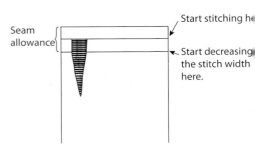

Seam allowance

Start stitching here

Start decreasing the stitch width here.

Not drawn to scale; enlarged for clarity

USING ZIPPERS IN YOUR QUILTS

Quilt: *Silent Reflection* (page 40)

If you want to include zippers in your quilts, start collecting old zippers from friends or buy them cheaply at thrift stores. Half-zippers work well for piping or bending around a shallow curve. Substitute whole zippers for fabric strips in string- and strip-pieced quilts. Use zippers and zipper pulls as an embellishment on quilts or tote bags. Make jewelry with zippers. The ideas go on and on.

TIP

Working with Zippers

- Use a zipper foot to stitch half or whole zippers in place.

- Cut zipper tape ravels easily. Zigzag the ends or use fabric glue to stop the fraying.

Zippers used in the quilt *Silent Reflection*:

White zipper

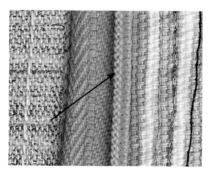

Yellow zipper

Green zipper

Other examples of using zippers:

Faultlines by Wendy Hill

Photo by Craig Howell

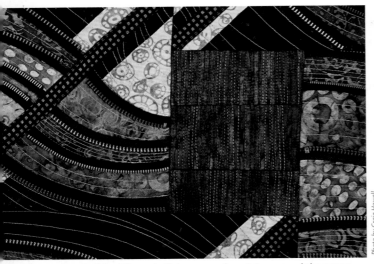

Photo by Craig Howell

Detail of *Faultlines*—half-zippers used as piping around the curves

Photo by Craig Howell

Detail of *Autumn Textures* (page 107). Whole zippers replace cut strips of fabric; zipper pulls add to the visual and physical texture of the composition.

1⅝″

Fold this edge to wrong side— ¼″ to ⅜″.

6″

Facing corner pattern

Fold this edge to wrong side—¼″ to ⅜″.

1⅝″

6″

More Challenge Quilts

In retrospect, Pat and I have always enjoyed participating in challenges. When the timing is right and the challenge theme inspires an idea, it's really fun to explore and exploit the given theme and rules.

QUILTS BY WENDY

Ugly Fabric Challenge

This is my very first challenge quilt, made in response to the Pine Tree Quilt Guild Ugly Fabric challenge. We traded 1-yard pieces of ugly fabric, hidden in a brown paper bag. With one simple rule—add up to three more pieces of fabric—you'd wonder how I managed to be disqualified at the Big Reveal. The Guild judges said I had "cheated" because I overdyed my ugly fabric and a solid white fabric to get several more values.

Cube Fantasy
by Wendy Hill,
34" × 29"

Scrap Bag Challenge

I bought a three-dollar scrap bag at a local fabric store. I challenged myself to make a quilt using only fabrics found in the overstuffed scrap bag plus the scraps in my own "tub o' scraps." (I have only one giant tub, while Pat has several colorful tubs.) I took a vacation from my usual approach and just started making units. I kept making units and design decisions as I went, which is more like the way Pat works. When I ran out of fabric from the scrap bag, I quit.

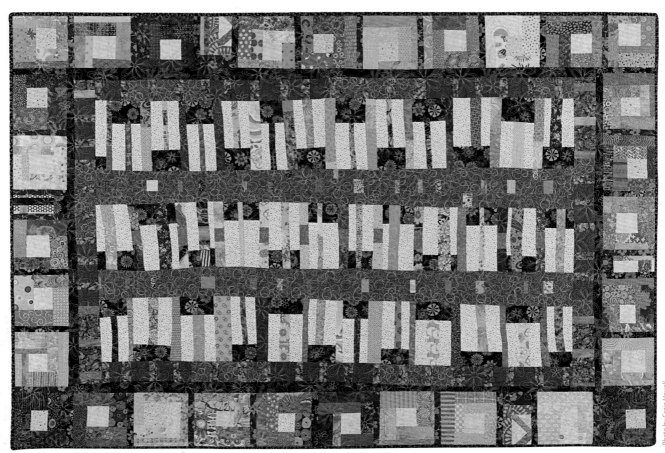

Happy Magic **by Wendy Hill,** 67" × 46"

Photo by Craig Howell

Dreaming in Dimensions Challenge

Timeless Treasures and C&T Publishing posed this challenge in 2005. My response to the challenge was constructed with various sizes of doughnut rings, scalloped on the outside edge, connected like the rings of a parking garage ramp. I used fast2fuse (by C&T Publishing; see Resources, page 111), a double-sided fusible stiff product, in the middle. The quilt is interactive, changing form each time it is installed.

Sea Form by Wendy Hill, 10″ × 10″ × 4″ in a bowl shape; various sizes installed

Zipper Challenge

I challenged myself to use zippers as a material to replace cut strips of fabric, as in strip piecing. As a result of a request for zippers in our electric co-op magazine, I received more than 90 packages of zippers from places ranging from Alaska to Arizona. Seeing the zippers sorted by color in grocery bags, I knew I had to use primarily zippers in a quilt.

Photo by Craig Howell

Autumn Textures by Wendy Hill, 41″ × 27″

QUILTS BY PAT

Color Cascade Challenge

Wendy and I belonged to a sewing group with about twenty members. We decided to do a color challenge, using the Ultimate 3-in-1 Color Tool (by C&T Publishing). The rules: Our quilts had to be exactly 18″ × 40″ finished with a facing, and from ten feet away, they had to read as our assigned color. Our exhibit, Color Cascade, went first to the Pacific International Quilt Festival in 2010 and then on to QuiltWorks in Bend, Oregon, 2010; Quilt Fest of New Jersey VII, 2011; Quilters' Affair Invitational Special Exhibit in Sisters, Oregon, 2011; Fabric of Vision in Ashland, Oregon, 2011; and Alex Anderson's Quilting in the Garden, 2011.

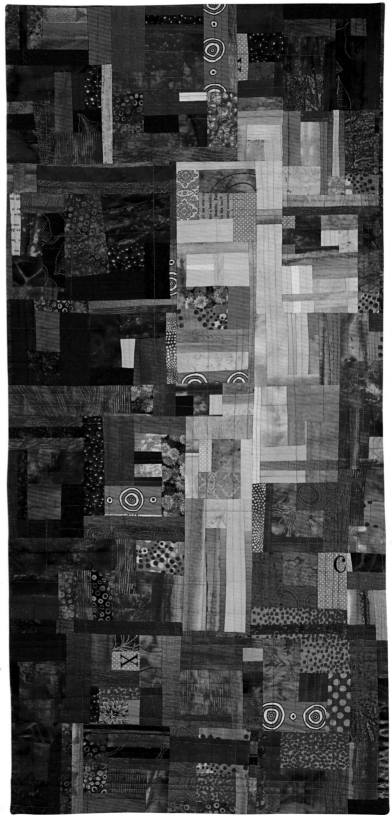

Photo by Craig Howell

Number 14 by Pat Pease, 18″ × 40″

Mountain Meadow Quilters Shaker Challenge

Frida was started in 2009 for a Mountain Meadow Quilters Shaker challenge, but it wasn't finished in time to be part of the exhibit. It has a string-pieced background with collaged parts on top. The real Frida is one of my four German wirehaired pointers, a Utility Prize I North American Versatile Hunting Dog Association champion and, to my mind, the best dog in the world.

Frida by Pat Pease, 36″ × 39″

Detail of *Frida*

Earth from Above Challenge

Our local central Oregon Studio Art Quilt Association issued an Earth from Above challenge. Other than size requirements, it was an open-ended challenge on this theme. This quilt is string-pieced, using hand-dyed fabrics and commercial cottons.

Beneath Me by Pat Pease, 18″ × 40″

Self Challenge

This is the first quilt I made using mostly contemporary Japanese cottons. I made blocks, one after the other, without regard to size or exact shape (most are not true squares). Instead of sewing the blocks together in rows and columns, I start piecing them into larger units and even larger units, until I had a quilt top. I trimmed the edges or added filler strips as needed to make the units fit together. It came out too long, so I cut off the bottom of the quilt, just like that. Much of the quilt is made up of home decor–weight linen fabrics, so it is quite heavy.

Put a Bird on It by Pat Pease, 52″ × 76″

Photo by Gary Alvis

ABOUT THE AUTHORS

Wendy and Pat

Pat started the creative process at an early age; her very talented craftsman father took her under his wing, and together they examined and created many things. Their travels around the United States and Canada helped to open Pat's mind and allow her to become a better observer. They always stopped at science, art, and history museums, and she remains

grateful for those experiences. About twelve years ago she made her first quilt and has yet to stop.

Wendy started making stuff at a very young age, first doing arts and crafts with her father and later sewing with her mother. She's been making things ever since. In fact, she calls herself a *maker*—someone who makes sense of our world through the creative process. Her first magazine article was published in 1992, and her articles have continued to appear to this day. This is her fifth book with C&T Publishing.

Pat and Wendy Together

When Pat and Wendy began collaborating, they couldn't know then how their very first

challenge—Unconventional Materials with supplies found at a grocery store—would change the direction of their lives.

As friends Pat and Wendy have a lot in common, but the ways they absorb information and approach design are quite different. It's exactly this push and pull and give and take that makes it fun for them to share their love of fabric as they develop their individual ideas into finished quilts.

Also available by Wendy Hill:

RESOURCES

Thread, Adhesives, and Stabilizers

American and Efird   amefird.com

Maxi-Lock, Mettler, Signature machine quilting thread, and other products

Aurifil   aurifil.com

Cotton and polyester thread and other products

Coats and Clark   makeitcoats.com

Coats and Clark Basting and Machine Embroidery Bobbin Thread and more for sewing, quilting, crocheting, knitting, needlework, and crafts

Kreinik   kreinik.com

Thread, accessories, kits, and more

Sulky of America   sulky.com

Sulky Blendables thread 12-weight and 30-weight; Sulky KK 2000 Temporary Spray Adhesive; and the water-soluble foundations Sulky Solvy, Sulky Super Solvy, Sulky Ultra Solvy, Sulky Paper Solvy, Sulky Fabri-Solvy, and Sulky Sticky Fabri-Solvy

Superior Threads   superiorthreads.com

Vanish water-soluble thread in two thicknesses, Vanish-Extra and Vanish-Lite

Fabrics, Notions, and Paint

Dear Stella   dearstelladesign.com

Confetti Dot and other unique fabrics with modern style

Fiber on a Whim   fiberonawhim.com

Fabrics, paints, dyes, thread, fibers, beads, buttons, stamps, embellishments, and more

Ghee's   ghees.com

Zippers and other classic and unusual notions, patterns, and more

Oakshott Fabrics   oakshottfabrics.com

Iridescent shot cottons

Quilters Dream
quiltersdreambatting.com

Batting

Ranger Industries   rangerink.com

Tim Holtz Distress Paint, inks, embossing powders, stamp pads, tools, paper crafting supplies, and more

Seed to Sewer: Akonye Kena   akonyekena.com > See: Fabric Dyeing—Seed to Sewer

"Seed to sewer" fabrics, all produced in accordance with fair trade guidelines

Timeless Treasures   ttfabrics.com

Sketch Basic and other fabric collections

Books and Other Products

C&T Publishing   ctpub.com

Joen Wolfrom's Magic Design-Ratio Tool; Ultimate 3-in-1 Color Tool, Updated 3rd Edition; Make It Simpler Fusible Interfacing; fast2fuse Double-Sided Fusible Stiff Interfacing (in Light, Medium, or Heavy)